Table of Contents

Author's Notes	1
Introduction	2
Shopping List	3
Gluten List	4
Breakfast	5
Sidekicks	17
Main Course	41
Desserts, Snacks, and Beverages	75
Seasonings, Sauces, and Dressings	88
Index	94

Author's Notes

Before committing to a gluten-free lifestyle, please consult your doctor. The information provided in this book is not intended to be a substitute for an individual's diet or medical advice in diagnosing or treating a health problem.

Always double check the ingredient list each time you buy an item, even if you were assured the item was gluten-free previously; manufactures may change their ingredients and process without notice. The author assumes no liability for any inaccuracies, misstatements, opinions, comments, ingredients or products in this book.

All cooking times are approximate and may vary according to skill, appliances, preparations and other cooking conditions.

Abbreviations:

TBS   Tablespoon
tsp   Teaspoon
GF   Gluten-free

Heather Demeritte's
Gluten Free & Dairy Free for the Frugal and Lazy Cook

by Heather Demeritte

a cookbook series
dedicated to
gluten-free, dairy-free living

Visit Us at:
www.GlutenFreeAndFrugal.com

Gluten-Free & Frugal

Loving Food on a Restrictive Diet

Dedicated to my amazing designer, photographer, editor, publisher, and husband T. Demeritte, Jr. for his creative ideas and encouragement.

original printing 2009

© Gluten-Free & Frugal 2010 All rights reserved.
Photos and content may not be republished, broadcast, rewritten or redistributed without written permission from the publisher.

p.Edition
E-created in 2013 by
The Frugal & Lazy Cook
available for download on Kindle and Apple's iBookstore

™

Scottsdale, AZ

* The creators of this book produced the majority of photography. Some stock photos were used to better represent a few images.

Introduction:

When I discovered that I had to strictly abstain from gluten and dairy due to celiac disease, I was faced with a dilemma. I could: A: Panic and dramatically cry out that I am going to starve and mournfully reflect the loss of enjoying pizza, raisin bran cereal, and ice cream; or B: Eat them anyway and face the ultimate consequences of a gastronomical ailment; or C: Find new delicious ways to enjoy gluten and dairy-free meals for my family and me.

I chose C.

I cook, not only as a means to sustain life, but also as a hobby to explore the culinary art of creating edible masterpieces. I knew in order to restore my health and regain peace with my body after years of suffering physical distress, malnutrition, and mental blur, I would have to adapt a new lifestyle that requires a restricted diet.

I set out to collect recipes dedicated to a gluten, dairy-free lifestyle, but I was extremely disappointed that most recipes called for an endless list of strange, expensive ingredients, with hours of preparation. Who has the time or money? Not me. But I was determined not to starve. So I created healthy recipes that are naturally gluten and dairy-free, easy to make, and affordable. From carnivores to vegetarians, chefs to "water-burners," or those who can eat anything to those who can't, each will equally enjoy my recipes.

In my compilation, some ingredients are store-bought items such as gluten-free bread, rice pasta, and prepackaged sauces, however, all the recommended ingredients and products are nutritious and contribute to a healthy, wholesome lifestyle. If you are the Betty Crocker of the gluten-free world, feel free to substitute your own baking wonders for those bought in a store. As for the frugal student, busy parent, and inexperienced cook, take advantage of the ever-expanding shelves in your local grocery store of gluten, dairy-free items. Stock up by following the shopping list on page 3 and never fret over what you are going to eat today.

Just because you have to live a restrictive life, doesn't mean you are restricted from enjoying life. So love the food that you eat, even if it is gluten-free or dairy-free.

Shopping List

For product recommendations visit www.glutenfreeandfrugal.com

Meats, Poultry, Fish, Egg, Beans, Legumes
Ground turkey, chicken or lean beef
Chicken breast
Turkey sausage, without fillers*
Deli meat*
Frozen fish, salmon, any white-fleshed fish
Frozen shrimp
Canned tuna and salmon*
Cage-free eggs
Silken and extra-firm tofu
*Beware of packaged or processed meats because they may contain gluten or lactose

Milk Alternatives
Plain flavored soy, almond, hazelnut, or rice milk
Vanilla flavored soy, almond, hazelnut, or rice milk
Soy cheese slices
Shredded soy cheese
Soy yogurt, plain or fruit flavored

Vegetables
Use frozen, unless otherwise noted, but fresh is ok too
Frozen vegetables
Pre-cut baby carrots
Fresh spinach, romaine, and kale leaves
Bell pepper, green, red, or yellow
Celery
Green onions
Potatoes
Frozen diced or shredded hash browns
Acorn, butternut, spaghetti squash
Zucchini
Canned mushrooms (without added ingredients)
Canned tomatoes, diced and stewed
Fresh Roma (plum) tomato

Fruits
Try to select organic as much as possible
Apples
Applesauce, jarred
Avocado
Banana
Cranberries, dried, fresh or frozen
Grapefruit
Grapes
Pears
Peaches
Raisins
Canned pineapple, in own juice

Grains
GF bread of choice
GF rice spaghetti
Brown rice, instant or dry
GF rice flour
Quinoa
Instant polenta
Puffed rice cereal

Baking goods
GF cornstarch
Honey
Agave syrup
Maple syrup
sugar, white and brown
Dark chocolate

Nuts and seeds
Flaxseed
Pumpkin seeds
nuts
nut butters, peanut or almond

Spices
Use dried, unless noted. Substitute 1 tsp. dried for 1 TBS fresh. If using dried, check to make sure it is gluten-free
Frozen vegetables
Pre-cut baby carrots
Fresh spinach, romaine, and kale leaves
Bell pepper, green, red, or yellow
Celery
Green onions
Potatoes
Frozen diced or shredded hash browns
Acorn, butternut, spaghetti squash
Zucchini
Canned mushrooms (without added ingredients)
Canned tomatoes, diced and stewed
Fresh Roma (plum) tomato

Oils, Condiments,
Extra-virgin olive oil (use for dressing)
Canola oil, use for high temperature cooking
GF BBQ sauce
GF salsa
GF marinara

Beverages
Apple cider
Black and green tea, decaf or regular
Cranberry juice

Gluten List

This is a partial list of gluten and non-gluten items. An expanded list can be found at www.glutenfreeandfrugal.com. I am not a doctor, so please consult your doctor before beginning a gluten-free diet.

Foods to Avoid
Wheat
Barley
Rye
Oat *
Malt
Couscous
Dorum
Spelt
Triticale
Matzo meal
Kamut Bulgar
Farina
Semolina
Einkorn
Farro
Graham flour

*The issue with oat products is not the grain but the manufacturing process. When oats are processed in the same facilities as wheat, contamination can occur. Oat products can be found that are not cross contaminated Consult your doctor before introducing oats to a GF diet.

Many foods made from grains contain gluten (unless they are labeled gluten-free or processed in a facility free from gluten) such as:
Breads, crackers and croutons
Cereals
Pasta
Cookies, cakes and pies
Soups
Gravies
Sauces (including soy sauce)
Salad dressings
Beer
Candy

*This also includes: Imitation, self basting, and processed meat or seafood, and food additives, such as malt flavoring and modified food starch.

Foods Allowed
Rice
Potato
Corn
Quinoa
Tapioca
Millet
Buckwheat
Yam
Teff
Amaranth
Arrowroot flour
Gelatin
Xanthan gum
Guar gum
Sorghum
Fresh meats, fish, poultry
 *Should NOT include; breaded, batter-coated, or marinated items.
Most dairy
*can be included (if not lactose intolerant)
Fruits
 *fresh, frozen or canned in juice, plain dried fruit
Vegetables
*includes; fresh, frozen, or canned
Nuts
Wine and distilled liquors, ciders, and spirits
*Alcohol beverages are included with great caution because manufacturing can significantly vary, sometimes including items that should be avoided.

Always double check ingredient lists, and if in doubt, leave it out!

Breakfast

Banana Nut Smoothie 6
Orange-Strawberry Slush 7
Crunchy Fruit Parfait 8
Honey-Walnut Poached Pears 9
Quinoa Breakfast Porridge 10
The Versatile French Toast 11
Quick Breakfast Burrito 12
Fast Spanish Tortilla 13
Southwestern Tofu Scramble on Toast 14
Egg in the Window 15
Sausage Pepper-Potato Sauté 16

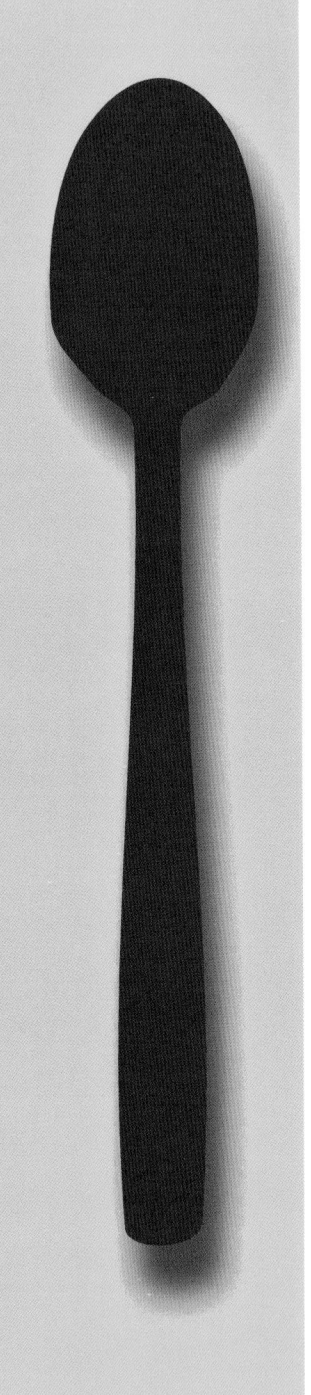

Banana Nut Smoothie

Enjoy this as a delicious, on-the-go breakfast or a healthy, fulfilling snack. Freeze the bananas in advance.

Serves: 2
Approximate Time: 5 minutes

Ingredients:
2 cups vanilla flavored milk alternative
2 medium frozen bananas, peeled
4 TBS peanut butter
1/2 cup ice (*more if needed*)
2 tsp. natural sweetener, such as honey, agave syrup or stevia (*optional*)

Directions:
1. Add all the ingredients in the blender and mix until everything resembles a smooth texture. *Each blender is different.*
2. Serve immediately into two tall glasses.

Variation Tips:
Be creative and add strawberries or substitute almond butter for the peanut butter.

Orange-Strawberry Slush

This cool, refreshing version of juice has a chilly twist.

Serves: 4 (about 1 cup)
Approximate Time: 5 minutes

Ingredients:
2 oranges, peeled and sectioned
1 ½ **cups** orange juice
1 ½ **cups** frozen or fresh strawberries
1 **TBS** honey
½ **cup** ice (double the amount if using fresh strawberries)

Directions:
1. Place the **oranges, juice, strawberries,** and **honey** into a blender; blend until smooth while adding ice.
2. Strain into 4 glasses.

Nutrition Tip:
You can amplify the protein by adding 1 scoop of protein powder or increase the fiber by adding 2 TBS of flaxseed while blending.

Crunchy Fruit Parfait

You can use any flavor of lactose-free yogurt and any variety of fruit to create your own parfait

Serves: 4
Approximate Time: 10 minutes

Ingredients:
2 cups of GF puffed rice cereal
2 TBS honey, softened (*see tip below*)
2 cups soy yogurt, any flavor
2 cups fresh fruit, blueberries, strawberries etc.

Directions:
1. In a small bowl mix **cereal** with **honey**, until fully coated; add more honey if needed.
2. In each bowl, scoop **1/4 cup** of **honey cereal mixture**, **1/4 cup** of **yogur**t, then **1/4 cup** of **fruit**; repeat with **1/4 cup** of **honey-cereal** mixture, **1/4 cup** of **yogurt** and top with remaining **fruit.**
3. Serve immediately.

Cooking Tip:
When measuring with honey, coat the measuring cup with non-stick spray. To soften honey, place the measured amount in a small glass container and microwave on high for 10-15 seconds, stirring after every 5 seconds. Be careful not to let it boil or scorch the honey. Immediately mix the cereal with the warmed honey.

Honey-Walnut Poached Pears

This can be served as a fulfilling, nutritious breakfast or enjoyed as a delectable dessert.

Serves: 4 (8 slices each)
Approximate Time: 20 minutes

Ingredients:
3 **TBS** honey
2 **TBS** lemon juice
1 **tsp.** cinnamon
1 ½ **cups** water
4 firm pears
2 **TBS** walnut slices

Directions:
1. Heat the **honey, lemon juice, cinnamon,** and **water** in a pan; boil for 10 minutes or until water is reduced to half.
2. Slice the **pears** into eighths; discard cores.
3. Place pears in the syrup mixture and gently simmer, about 5 minutes or until the pears are tender.
4. Transfer to a serving bowl; can be served warm or chilled.
5. Garnish with **walnut slices**.

Nutritional Tip:
Pears are full of vitamin C and fiber and are at their seasonal best during the autumn months.

Quinoa Breakfast Porridge

The Incas call quinoa (pronounced KEEN-wah) "mother of all grains", which deserves the title since it richly supplies vitamins, minerals, and protein.

Serves: 4
Approximate Time: 7 minutes

Ingredients: **2 cups** cooked quinoa (*see tip below*)
1 cup milk alternative (*or more depending on desired consistency*)
1 TBS honey
2 tsp. cinnamon
1 cup dried or fresh fruit such as bananas, raisins, etc.
¼ cup sliced almonds

Directions:
1. In a saucepan, combine prepared **quinoa** with **milk alternative**, **honey**, and **cinnamon**; bring to a simmer and stir frequently for 5 minutes, or until cereal thickens.
2. Remove from heat and stir in **fruit** and **nuts**; cover and allow it to sit for 2 minutes.
3. Equally serve in 4 bowls; garnish with additional honey, if desired.

Cooking Tip:
If you don't have leftover quinoa, prepare according to package and begin with the first step during the last five minutes of cooking time.

The Versatile French Toast

This basic recipe opens a wide variety of breakfast options.
(See tip)

Serves: 4 (2 slices each)
Approximate Time: 10 minutes

Ingredients:
2 eggs or 3 egg whites
1 cup of vanilla flavored milk alternative
¼ tsp. of cinnamon
1 tsp. of raw sugar *(optional)*
8 slices of GF bread

Directions:
1. Break **eggs** into a wide, shallow bowl and gently beat with a fork until soft peaks form.
2. Stir in the **milk alternative**, **cinnamon**, and **sugar**.
3. Spray a skillet with non-stick cooking spray and heat over medium high heat.
4. Dip both sides of each **bread** slice in the mixture and carefully transfer to the hot skillet.
5. Brown on both sides 1 to 2 minutes or until golden brown.

Variation Tip:
Vermont Style: Serve with maple syrup.
Snow Top: Dust with powdered sugar.
Berry Tasty: Top with fresh berries.
Apple-licious: Spread warm Honey-Spiced Applesauce (page 80) on top or between slices.
Crazy Shapes: Use cookie cutters to create fun shapes.
Honey Nut: Pour warm honey and sprinkle with chopped walnuts.
Nutty Monkey: Smooth nut butter on one side of each slice, and place sliced bananas between slices.
Perfect Pear-wich: Place the Honey-Almond Poached Pears (page 9) between slices or on top.

Quick Breakfast Burrito

Although I call this a breakfast burrito, I usually eat it for a quick lunch with a salad of mixed greens topped with extra salsa.

Serves: 4

Approximate Time: 10 minutes

Ingredients:
4 eggs lightly beaten
1 tsp. oregano
dash cayenne pepper (*optional*)
1 (2 oz.) can green chilies
¼ cup onions, chopped
4 corn tortillas
½ cup shredded soy cheese (*optional*)
1/2 cup salsa (*or use recipe on pg. 93*)

Directions:
1. Beat **eggs** with **oregano** and **cayenne pepper.**
2. Spray a skillet with non-stick cooking spray and heat over medium heat; add **egg mixture**, **green chilies**, and **onions**; constantly scramble until eggs are set.
3. Evenly serve into each **tortilla;** sprinkle **cheese** atop eggs and roll up, and replace the tortilla back into the skillet, folded side down; cook for 1 minute or until slightly charred.
4. Carefully flip the burrito to grill the other side for 1 minute.
5. Serve with **salsa.**

Cooking Tip:
To keep the tortilla from unrolling in the skillet place a spoon on top while it is cooking.

Fast Spanish Tortilla

In Spain a tortilla is a potato-based omelet. Use refrigerated shredded hash browns in place of the traditional diced potatoes to save time.

Serves: 6
Approximate Time: 25 minutes

Ingredients:
6 eggs
1 TBS oil
2 ½ cups of shredded hash browns (*see tip below for fresh potatoes*)
   salt and pepper to taste
1/2 cup shredded soy cheese
1/3 cup salsa (*or use recipe on pg. 93*)
shredded lettuce and carrots, *optional*

Directions:
1. Whisk **eggs** in a bowl; set aside.
2. Heat **oil** over medium heat in a large ovenproof skillet.
3. Add **potatoes** and sprinkle with salt and pepper; cook for 5 minutes or until potatoes are lightly browned.
4. Mash potatoes in the skillet.
5. Evenly pour the eggs over the potatoes.
6. Cook uncovered for 5 minutes, tilting the skillet and lifting the edges of the eggs with a spatula to allow yolk to run underneath.
7. Turn broiler on; broil the omelet 4 to 5 inches from the broiler for 2 minutes, or until top is set.
8. Sprinkle **cheese** and let stand for 5 minutes.
9. Cut into six wedges and serve with **salsa** on a bed of **lettuce** and **carrots**.

Cooking Tip:
If you choose to use fresh potatoes, dice the potatoes as small as possible and fry 10 to 15 minutes before adding the egg. If you want to reduce the cholesterol and fat in the recipe, use 3 whole eggs and six egg whites or 1 carton (15 oz.) of egg replacement.

Southwestern Tofu Scramble on Toast

Try this egg alternative to a traditional southwestern breakfast.

Serves: 4
Approximate Time: 5 minutes

Ingredients:
1 tsp. oil
1 cup frozen corn, (can use fresh)
1 (12 oz.) package extra-firm tofu (pat-dry and mashed)
½ cup salsa *(or use recipe on pg. 93)*
¼ cup green onion, chopped
   Salt and pepper to taste
4 slices GF bread

Direction:
1. Heat **oil** in a skillet; add **corn** and **tofu** and stir until heated thorough.
2. Stir in **salsa**, reduce heat, and cook for 1 minute more; sprinkle with **salt** and **pepper.**
3. Toast **bread** and serve tofu mixture and **green onions** on top.

Variation Tip:
Eat breakfast for dinner and wrap the tofu mixture in a warm corn tortilla and serve with a Mediterranean Salad on page 27 and Creamy Pea Soup on page 33.

Egg in the Window

This is an easy variation of the classic English breakfast.

Serves: 4
Approximate Time: 10 minutes

Ingredients:
4 slices GF bread
4 eggs

Directions:
1. Cut a square in the the middle of each slice of **bread;** save for later.
2. Spray a skillet with non-stick cooking spray; layer each slice in skillet over medium heat.
3. Break an **egg** inside the square of each slice.
4. Wait for the egg to harden before carefully turning it over with a wide spatula.
5. Once the yolk is cooked (about 2 minutes), slide your Egg-in-the-Window onto a plate.

Variation Tip:
Keep the cut-out slice and toast in skillet, then place on top of cooked egg. Have fun and use a cookie cutter to make different shapes.

Sausage Pepper-Potato Sauté

This hearty breakfast-based meal can be served as a light dinner as well.

Serves: 4
Approximate Time:

Ingredients:
1 TBS oil
1 lb. small yellow potatoes, cubed
1/2 cup red bell pepper (1 medium), thinly sliced
1/2 cup onion (1 small), cut into 8 wedges
4 turkey sausage links, cut into fourths
Salt and pepper to taste

Directions:
1. Heat **oil** in a skillet over medium heat; add the **potatoes** and **bell peppers** and sauté for about 7 minutes.
2. Add **onion** and continue to sauté for about 5 minutes or until veggies are slightly tender; remove from skillet and set aside.
3. Add the **sausage** to the skillet and cook until browned, about five minutes.
4. Add the pepper-potato mixture to the sausage in the skillet.
5. Sprinkle **salt** and **pepper**; stir well and serve.

Health Tip:
Using turkey sausage helps lower the cholesterol and fat content.

Side Kicks

Cajun Sweet Potato Fries 18
Baked Acorn Squash 19
Onion-Pepper Sauté 20
Roasted Asparagus 21
Sesame Stir-Fry Green Beans 22
Italian Spaghetti Squash 23
Stove Top Rosemary Potatoes 24
Tuscany Broccoli 25
Honey-Mustard Side Salad 26
Mediterranean Salad 27
Cranberry Walnut Wild Rice 28
Fried Rice 29
Simple Spanish Rice 30
Oven Baked Croutons 31
Cranberry Soup 32
Creamy Pea Soup 33
Italian Minestrone Soup 34
Pumpkin Soup 35
Spicy Tomato Soup 36
Chinese Chicken Soup 37
Chicken Noodless Soup 38
Creamy Lentil Soup 39
Curry Cauliflower and Broccoli Soup 40

Cajun Sweet Potato Fries

A spicy version of typical steak fries with a southern flare.

Serves: 4
Approximate Time: 30

Ingredients:

1 lb. sweet potatoes,
2 tsp. oil
3 tsp. Cajun seasoning *(or use recipe on pg. 89)*

Directions:

1. Preheat oven to 450 degrees F.
2. Slice the **potatoes** into ¼ inch wedges with skins on.
3. Combine **oil** and **seasoning** in a large bowl.
4. Add the potatoes and mix thoroughly into seasoning mixture.
5. Spray a large cookie sheet with non-stick cooking spray; evenly layer the potatoes on the sheet.
6. Bake for 20 to 25 minutes, or until slightly crispy on the outside but tender in the inside.

Timesaving Tip:

To save baking time, pierce the potatoes and microwave for 3 minutes, or until it still has a slight resistance when pierced with a fork. Then proceed with baking, subtracting at least 10 minutes of baking time.

Baked Acorn Squash

This favorable winter squash tastes great with baked chicken, pork chops, or roast beef.

Serves: 4
Approximate Time: 30 minutes

Ingredients:
1 lb. acorn squash (2 small)
2 TBS oil
1 TBS Italian seasoning *(or use recipe on pg. 90)*

Directions:
1. Preheat oven to 450 degrees F.
2. Spray baking pan with nonstick cooking spray.
3. Cut **acorn** in half and scoop out the seeds and discard; slice into 8 wedges.
4. Place squash in pan (flesh-side up).
5. Mix **oil** and **seasoning** in a small bowl and pour over squash. Use a brush to evenly spread the mixture.
6. Bake for 25 minutes or until tender.

Timesaving Tip:
You can boil the squash for 5 minutes prior to putting them in the oven to decrease baking time up to 10 minutes.

Cajun Sweet Potato Fries

A spicy version of typical steak fries with a southern flare.

Serves: 4
Approximate Time: 30

Ingredients:

1 lb. sweet potatoes,
2 tsp. oil
3 tsp. Cajun seasoning *(or use recipe on pg. 89)*

Directions:

1. Preheat oven to 450 degrees F.
2. Slice the **potatoes** into ¼ inch wedges with skins on.
3. Combine **oil** and **seasoning** in a large bowl.
4. Add the potatoes and mix thoroughly into seasoning mixture.
5. Spray a large cookie sheet with non-stick cooking spray; evenly layer the potatoes on the sheet.
6. Bake for 20 to 25 minutes, or until slightly crispy on the outside but tender in the inside.

Timesaving Tip:

To save baking time, pierce the potatoes and microwave for 3 minutes, or until it still has a slight resistance when pierced with a fork. Then proceed with baking, subtracting at least 10 minutes of baking time.

Baked Acorn Squash

This favorable winter squash tastes great with baked chicken, pork chops, or roast beef.

Serves: 4
Approximate Time: 30 minutes

Ingredients:
1 lb. acorn squash (2 small)
2 TBS oil
1 TBS Italian seasoning *(or use recipe on pg. 90)*

Directions:
1. Preheat oven to 450 degrees F.
2. Spray baking pan with nonstick cooking spray.
3. Cut **acorn** in half and scoop out the seeds and discard; slice into 8 wedges.
4. Place squash in pan (flesh-side up).
5. Mix **oil** and **seasoning** in a small bowl and pour over squash. Use a brush to evenly spread the mixture.
6. Bake for 25 minutes or until tender.

Timesaving Tip:
You can boil the squash for 5 minutes prior to putting them in the oven to decrease baking time up to 10 minutes.

Onion-Pepper Sauté

This rustic side only needs four ingredients and 10 minutes!

Serves: 4
Approximate Time: 10 minutes

Ingredients:
1 tsp. oil
1/2 cup onion (1 small), cut in wedges
2 medium green bell peppers, sliced into thin strips
3 tsp. basil

Directions
1. Heat **oil** over medium-high.
2. Add the **onion;** sauté for 1 minute.
3. Add the **bell pepper** slices and sauté for 5 minute or until the vegetables are soft.
4. Sprinkle **basil** and quickly stir to coat.
5. Serve immediately.

Timesaving Tip:
To save a few minutes of preparation, use frozen onions, adding them two minutes *after* you sautéed the bell peppers.

Roasted Asparagus

Enjoy this delicious side dish that will surely delight everyone.

Serves: 4
Approximate Time: 15 minutes

Ingredients:
1 lb. asparagus *(if frozen, thaw completely)*
1 tsp. oil
2 garlic cloves, finely chopped
¼ tsp. salt, *if desired*

Directions:
1. Preheat oven to 500 degrees F.
2. Lightly coat baking sheet with non-stick cooking spray
3. Cut the woody ends of **asparagus,** if necessary.
4. Arrange in a single layer on the sheet.
5. In a small bowl, combine **oil** and **garlic;** drizzle evenly over the asparagus; season with **salt.**
6. Roast for 5 minutes. Shake the pan to toss the asparagus; cook for an additional 3 to 5 minutes or until tender.

Variation Tip:
You can top the asparagus with lemon-flavored soy yogurt or make your own by mixing 6 oz. plain soy yogurt with 1 tsp. of lemon.

Sesame Stir-Fry Green Beans

This Chinese side dish is a delicious compliment to a chicken and fried rice dinner.

Serves: 4
Approximate Time: 15 minutes

Ingredients:
1 tsp. oil
1 garlic clove, chopped
4 cups frozen green beans *(if using fresh see tip below)*
1 tsp. teriyaki sauce *(or use recipe on pg. 92)*
1 TBS sesame seed

Directions:
1. Heat **oil** over medium heat; sauté **garlic**.
2. Add **green beans** and cook until fully heated through.
3. Slowly pour **teriyaki sauce**; mix well.
4. Toss with **sesame seeds**.
5. Serve warm.

Cooking Tip:
If using fresh green beans, steam or cook the green beans in a small amount of water until al dente. Drain before adding to skillet. Steaming retains most of the nutrients.

Italian Spaghetti Squash

Satisfy your craving for spaghetti with this vegetable-based "pasta" alongside Roasted Zucchini and Fish on page 66.

Serves: 4
Approximate Time: 30 minutes

Ingredients:
2 lb. spaghetti squash (1 large)
1/2 cup water or broth
1 cup marinara sauce *(or use recipe on pg. 92)*
   salt and pepper to taste

Directions:
1. Cut the **squash** in half, lengthwise; scoop out seeds.
2. Place 1/2 cup **water** in roasting pan, place cut side down and bake until a sharp knife can be inserted with a little resistance; set aside to cool slightly.
3. Meanwhile, over medium heat reheat **marinara sauce** until heated through.
4. When the squash is cool enough, use a large spoon to scoop out the stringy pulp from the flesh; place on four plates.
5. Top with warm marinara sauce.

Variation Tip:
Substitute the marinara sauce and use Ratatouille (pg. 56) or serve topped with Savory Meatballs (pg. 54)

Stove Top Rosemary Potatoes

This quick side dish saves you time when you cook potatoes on the stove instead of roasting or baking.

Serves: 4
Approximate Time: 15 minutes

Ingredients:
1 TBS oil, more if needed
2 garlic gloves, minced
2 lb. potatoes, diced with skins
½ cup water or broth, *more if needed*
1 TBS rosemary
   salt and pepper to taste

Directions:
1. Heat **oil** in pan over medium heat and sauté **garlic** for 30 seconds.
2. Add **potatoes** in a single layer and fully mix with oil.
3. Add **water** or **broth**, cover and cook, stirring occasionally for about 6 minutes or until most of the broth has disappeared.
4. Sprinkle **rosemary**, **salt** and **pepper**; stir to fully coat the potatoes. If the potatoes start to look dry, add more oil or water.
5. Cook uncovered frequently stirring until potatoes are golden brown on the outside and tender inside, about 2 minutes.
6. Serve immediately.

Cooking Tip:
The smaller the potatoes are cut up, the faster they cook. Any potato is fine to cook with, but keep the skins on to increase nutrient and fiber content.

Tuscany Broccoli

This side dish requires two steps and 5 minutes, but it tastes like it came straight from Italy.

Serves: 4
Approximate Time: 5 minutes

Ingredients:
1 tsp. oil
3 garlic cloves, minced
4 cups (1 lb.) frozen broccoli florets
1 tsp. marjoram
¼ tsp. red pepper flakes
   salt and pepper to taste

Directions:
1. Heat **oil** in a large skillet over medium heat, sauté **garlic** for 30 seconds.
2. Add **broccoli, marjoram, red pepper flakes, salt** and **pepper**; sauté until broccoli is tender, about 3 minutes.

Menu Tip:
Enjoy this side dish with Grilled Chicken Pomodoro (*pg. 45*) and a light white wine for a simple, yet eloquent dinner.

Honey Mustard Side Salad

This basic salad can compliment any dish and can serve as a foundation for a variety of toppings and dressings

Serves: 4
Approximate Time: 10 minutes

Ingredients:
1 tsp. oil
1 garlic clove, sliced in half
8 cups mixed greens, washed *(see tip on page 27)*
¼ cup shredded carrots,
1 cucumber, sliced
1 tomato, sliced into wedges
¼ cup red onion (1 small)
¼ cup sunflower seeds
4 TBS honey mustard dressing *(or use recipe on pg. 91)*
½ cup gluten-free croutons *(or use recipe on pg. 31)*

Directions:
1. Smear **oil** in a large salad bowl; rub both halves of **garlic** on the side of the bowls; discard clove after use.
2. Toss **mixed greens** with **carrots**, **cucumbers**, **tomato**, **onion**, **sunflower seeds,** and **dressing**.
3. Top with **croutons**.

Variation Tip:
Mix in pine nuts, olives, or capers, if desired.

Mediterranean Salad

This simple and light salad can accompany any Greek, Italian, Spanish, Moroccan or French dish.

Serves: 4
Approximate Time: 5 minutes

Ingredients:
4 cups (1 lb.) fresh spinach
1 cucumber, seeded and sliced
½ cup (1/2 lb.) red onion, sliced
1 large tomato, sliced
1/2 cup black olives
3 TBS Mediterranean Dressing *(or use recipe on pg. 91)*
½ cup GF croutons *(or use recipe on pg. 31)*

Directions:
1. Toss **spinach, cucumber, onion, tomatoes,** and **olives** in a large bowl.
2. Drizzle the **dressing** over the top.
3. Top with **croutons**.

Cooking Tip:
Remove dirt from greens by swirling them around in a large bowl of salt water.

Cranberry-Walnut Wild Rice

Enjoy this crunchy and tart variation of rice.

Serves: 4
Approximate time: 10 minutes

Ingredients:
2 cups cooked wild rice, or prepare according to package
¼ cup rice wine vinegar
2 tsp. oil
1 tsp. black pepper
½ cup dried cranberries
½ cup chopped walnuts

Directions
1. Prepare **rice** or place cooked rice in saucepan over medium heat
2. Combine **rice wine vinegar, oil**, and **pepper** in a bowl.
3. Mix well with rice; cover and cook until heated through.
4. Add **cranberries** and **walnuts** and toss before serving.

Menu Tip:
Serve this beside Turkey with Herb and Onion Gravy (*pg. 48*).

Fried Rice

By using leftover rice and frozen vegetables, you can cook this healthier version of the classic fried rice in no time!

Serves: 4
Approximate Time: 10 minutes

Ingredients:
2 TBS oil, divided
3 cups brown rice, cooked
1 cup frozen peas and carrots, thawed
2 tsp GF soy sauce
1 egg plus **3** egg whites, lightly beaten in a small bowl
2 green onions, diced

Directions:
1. Heat the **oil** in the skillet, then add **rice**; stir to coat the rice with the oil, about 1 minute.
2. Reduce heat to medium-low and constantly stir until the rice is heated through, about 2 minutes.
3. Add the **peas**, **carrots** and **soy sauce** and thoroughly stir to combine.
4. Once the vegetables are heated, fold in the **egg mixture** and cook until eggs are fully heated; constantly stir to prevent the egg mixture from sticking to the pan.
5. Remove from stove and stir in the **green onions**.

Menu Tip:
Serve alongside Teriyaki Bowl (pg. 50)

Simple Spanish Rice

The subtle hint of chili powder and cumin creates an enticing flavor to this side dish.

Serves: 4
Approximate Time: 30 minutes

Ingredients:
2 TBS oil
3 garlic cloves, chopped
½ cup onion (3 oz.)
1 ½ cups uncooked rice, brown or white
1 ½ cups chicken or vegetable broth
1 (14.5 oz.) can tomatoes with juice, diced
1 (4 oz.) can green chilies
¾ tsp. chili powder
¾ tsp. oregano
1 tsp. cumin

Directions:
1. Heat **oil** in a skillet; sauté **garlic** and **onion**; cook until onion is softened about 1-2 minutes.
2. Add dry **rice**, stir until golden brown, about 2 minutes.
3. Slowly add **broth** and **tomatoes** with juice.
4. Stir in **green chilies, chili powder, oregano,** and **cumin**; bring to a boil.
5. Once boiling begins, reduce heat to low, cover and simmer for 20 minutes or until fluffy and liquid has been absorbed.
6. Remove from heat and allow it to sit for 5 minutes.

Cooking Tip:
Make sure the lid is tight, use foil if needed, and avoid lifting the lid while the rice is cooking.

Oven Baked Croutons

Add this to top a tossed salad or a soup.

Yields: 6 cups
Approximate Time: 20 minutes

Ingredients:
8 slices of GF bread of choice
2 TBS oil
2 cloves of garlic (minced)
1 TBS Italian seasoning *(or use recipe on pg. 90)*

Direction:
1. Preheat oven to 350 degrees F.
2. Remove crusts from the **bread slices**; cut into cubes.
3. In a large skillet, heat **oil** over medium heat; sauté **garlic** for 1 minute.
4. Turn off the heat and toss in **breadcrumbs** and **Italian seasoning** until fully coated.
5. Spread on a prepared baking sheet and bake for 15 minutes, or until crispy and dry; check frequently to prevent burning.

Cooking Tip:
You can refrigerate up to four days or freeze for three months.

Cranberry Soup

This burgundy hued soup is a sweet and tart appetizer before any poultry entree.

Serves: 4 (1 cup)
Approximate Time: 20 minutes

Ingredients:
3 cups fresh or frozen cranberries
4 cups water
1 cup applesauce
¼ tsp. cinnamon
¼ tsp. nutmeg
¼ tsp. black pepper
1 tsp. almond extract
2 TBS cornstarch

Directions:
1. Combine **cranberries** with **water, applesauce, cinnamon, nutmeg**, **pepper,** and **almond extract** in a large saucepan; bring to a boil, then reduce heat to low and cover; cook for 15 minutes
2. Pour soup in a blender and puree until smooth; replace into saucepan and bring to boil over medium heat.
3. Gradually add **cornstarch,** stirring constantly; cook for 5 minutes or until heated through.

Variation Tip:
Serve with crushed walnuts or a dollop of soy yogurt on top.

Creamy Pea Soup

The pureed potatoes make this soup so creamy and nutritiously delicious.

Serves: 4
Approximate Time: 15 minutes

Ingredients:
2 cups water or broth
½ lb. potato (1 medium) diced
4 cups frozen peas
   salt and pepper to taste

Directions:
1. Bring the **water** to a boil and add **potatoes**; reduce heat to medium and cook for 10 minutes or until tender.
2. Add **peas, salt** and **pepper**; simmer until heated through, about 2 minutes.
3. Pour into blender and puree until desired consistency; add more water if too thick.

Variation Tip:
You can add more flavor with spices, such as 1 tsp. of rosemary or thyme, or heat it up by sprinkling a pinch of cayenne pepper with cumin.

Italian Minestrone Soup

The traditional recipe calls for small pasta, but because of the abundance of vegetables and aromatic flavors of Italian spices, you wont even miss the pasta!

Serves: 4
Approximate Time: 30 minutes

Ingredients:

5 cups chicken or vegetable broth, divided
1/2 cup (3 oz.**)** onion, cut into wedges
5 garlic cloves minced
½ cup celery (2 stalks), diced
1 cup carrots (2 medium), peeled and diced
2 cups kale chopped
1 (15 oz.) can stewed whole tomatoes with juice
1 (15 oz.) can red beans
1 TBS dried Italian seasoning (*or use recipe on pg. 90*)
 salt and pepper to taste

Directions:

1. Heat 1/4 cup **broth** in a large soup pot over medium heat.
2. Add **onion** and stir frequently for about 5 minutes.
3. Add **garlic** and continue to stir for 1 minute.
4. Pour the remaining **broth** and the **celery, carrots,** and **kale.**
5. Reduce heat and cook uncovered for 15 minutes, or until vegetables are tender.
6. Add the **tomatoes** and **beans** and cook until heated through.
7. Sprinkle **Italian seasoning, salt** and **pepper** and serve.

Timesaving Tip:
Buy precut carrots to save preparation time.

Pumpkin Soup

My husband's grandmother altered for me this soup from the traditional cream-laden recipe to make the most delicious pumpkin soup I ever slurped! Although she used fresh pumpkin, I saved time by using canned.

Serves: 4 (1 1/4 cups)
Approximate Time: 10 minutes

Ingredients:
1 (29 oz.) can pure pumpkin
2 cups chicken broth
1/2 tsp. ground ginger
1/4 tsp. pepper, more if desired
1/4 tsp. nutmeg

Directions:
1. Combine all ingredients in a large pot over medium high heat. Be careful, soup will bubble.
2. Cover and simmer until heated through and it reached the desired thickness; add more water if too thick.
3. Serve warm in soup bowls with gluten-free toast.

Variation Tip:
Saute 1 chopped onion in 1 tsp. of oil before adding the remaining ingredients. Or add 1 cup applesauce, but omit ½ cup of broth.

Spicy Tomato Soup

A steaming and peppery soup that packs a double meaning to the word hot: it warms the soul while igniting the taste buds with fire!

Serves: 4

Approximate Time: 30 minutes

Ingredients:

1 TBS oil
½ cup celery (2 stalks), diced
½ cup onion (3 oz.), diced
2 cloves garlic, minced
1 (14 oz.) can diced tomatoes, with juice
1 cup chicken or vegetable broth
1 tsp. cumin
2 TBS cilantro
   red pepper flakes, to taste

Directions:
1. Heat **oil** over medium heat in a large, deep skillet.
2. Add the **celery, onion** and **garlic**; cook until vegetables are tender, about 1 minute.
3. Add the **tomatoes** with **juice**, **chicken broth**, **cumin, cilantro,** and **red pepper flakes.**
4. Simmer until vegetables are very tender, about 15 to 20 minutes.
5. Puree in blender until smooth.
6. Serve immediately in 4 bowls; garnish with fresh parsley leaves.

Menu Tip:
Serve this as an appetizer before Mediterranean Tuna Wrap (pg. 68) or sprinkle soy cheddar cheese just before serving.

Chinese Chicken Soup

This Far Eastern version of the traditional chicken noodle soup takes only 20 minutes from to start to finish to create!

Serves: 4
Approximate Time: 20 minutes

Ingredients:
8 oz. GF rice noodles
1 TBS oil
2 garlic cloves
1 tsp. ginger
6 cups chicken broth
1 medium green and red pepper, sliced
2 cups cooked skinless chicken breast, shredded
1 cup water chestnuts
red chili flakes *(optional)*

Directions:
1. Bring water to boil; cook **spaghetti** until al dente, about 10 minutes.
2. Meanwhile, in a skillet, heat **oil** over medium heat and sauté **garlic** about 1 minute; sprinkle **ginger**.
3. Add **broth** and bring to boil. Reduce heat and add **peppers, chicken,** and **chestnuts**; simmer about 5 minutes.
4. Drain noodles and divide into four bowls.
5. Ladle chicken soup over the noodles.
6. Sprinkle with desired amount of **red chili flakes**.

Variation Tip:
Add a can of rinsed mushrooms.

Chicken Noodle-less Soup

This warm, comforting soup can be made quickly with leftover chicken.

Serves: 4
Approximate Time: 20 minutes

Ingredients:
4 ½ **cups** chicken broth
½ **cup** white onion (3 oz.) chopped
1 **cup** carrots (3 medium) sliced
1/2 **cup** celery (2 stalks) sliced
1 (2 oz.) can of sliced mushrooms (rinsed)
1 **tsp.** basil
1 **tsp.** oregano
¼ **tsp.** black pepper
2 **cups** shredded cooked chicken

Directions:
1. Combine **broth** with **onion, carrots**, **celery**, **mushrooms** and **seasoning**: bring to a boil.
2. Add the **chicken**; reduce heat to medium and cook for 10 minutes.

Cooking Tip:
Chicken soup tastes better the next day, so make plenty of leftovers.

Creamy Lentil Soup

When my friend, Sherry, found out I couldn't tolerate milk, she offered this recipe. She used fresh veggies and 1 ½ cup of dry lentils, but I used frozen vegetables and canned lentils to save cooking time.

Serves: 4
Approximate Time: 15 minutes

Ingredients:
4 cups broth or water
3 cups carrots, chopped (can use frozen)
½ cup onion (3 oz.) chopped
½ cup celery (2 stalks), chopped
1 (15.5 oz.) can of lentils (drained and rinsed)
1 **tsp**. garlic (minced)
1 **tsp**. lemon juice
salt and pepper to taste

Directions:
1. In a large pot, combine **broth, carrots, onion,** and **celery;** bring to a boil and simmer until onions are clear.
2. Add the **lentils, garlic, lemon juice, salt** and **pepper;** simmer for 5 minutes, or until heated through.
3. Transfer soup to a blender and blend until creamy, adding more water if soup is too thick.
4. Return to pot and heat until ready to serve.

Menu Tip:
Serve this over a cup of cooked rice and garnish with fresh parsley to make it a complete vegetarian meal. Or serve it with gluten-free turkey sausage.

Curry Cauliflower and Broccoli Soup

The fragrant curry adds a delectable taste to please even the pickiest eaters.

Serves: 4 main dishes or 6 appetizers
Approximate Time: 25 minutes

Ingredients:
1 TBS oil
2 garlic cloves, minced
1 cup onion (1/2 lb.) diced
5 cups broth, chicken or vegetable, divided
4 cups (1 lb.) broccoli, fresh or frozen
4 cups (1 lb.) cauliflower, fresh or frozen
1 ½ tsp. curry powder
1/8 tsp. nutmeg
1 tsp. pepper
salt to taste

Directions:
1. Heat **oil** in a large pot over medium-high heat; sauté **garlic** and **onion** until translucent, about 2 minutes.
2. Add ¼ cup of **broth, broccoli,** and **cauliflower**; reduce heat and cover for about 5 minutes.
3. Add the remaining **broth**, **curry, nutmeg**, and **pepper**; simmer about 15 minutes or until vegetables are tender.
4. Transfer to a blender and puree until smooth.

Variation Tip:
You can add a little more kick to the soup by mixing in red pepper flakes.

Main Course

Asian Chicken and Brussels Sprouts 42
Classic Italian Grilled Chicken 43
Caribbean Chicken 44
Grilled Chicken Pomodoro 45
Three Ingredient Fiesta Chicken 46
Chinese Chicken Salad 47
Turkey with Herb and Onion Gravy 48
California Turkey Wrap 49
Teriyaki Bowl 50
Enchiladas with Homemade Sauce 51
Spicy Soft Tacos 52
Sloppy Jose' 53
Savory Meatballs 54
Chili with Beans 55
Ratatouille 56
Mushroom-Onion Burgers 57
Beef and Herb Potato Skillet 58
Tri-Pepper Beef Fajitas 59
Roast Beef Wrapped Asparagus 60
Broccoli and Sausage Pasta 61
Pepper-Jack Polenta Pizza 62
Garlicky-Lemon Salmon and Tomatoes 63
Fast Mediterranean Fish 64
Paprika Fish 65
Roasted Zucchini and Fish 66
Quinoa Shrimp Salad 67
Mediterranean Tuna Wrap 68
Quinoa Stuffed Peppers 69
Southwest Bean Burrito 70
Moroccan Chickpea Stew 71
Quickest Bean and Rice Meal 72
Mini Spinach-Mushroom Quesadilla 73
Portobello Chili-Melt 74

Asian Chicken and Brussels Sprouts

The subtle hint of ginger adds flavor to this Far Eastern dish.

Serves: 4
Approximate Time: 20 minutes

Ingredients:
1/3 cup soy sauce
1/3 cup rice vinegar
2 tsp. ground ginger
2 cups chicken broth
1 cup sliced carrots (about 3)
1 cup sliced celery (3 stalks)
1 ½ cups frozen Brussels sprouts
2 cups cooked shredded chicken breast
2 green onions, sliced

Directions:
1. Combine **soy sauce, rice vinegar, ginger**, and **chicken broth** in medium saucepan; bring to a boil.
2. Add **carrots, celery**, and **Brussels sprouts** and simmer for 6 minutes.
3. Add **chicken** and cook until chicken is heated through, about 2 minutes.
4. Divided into 4 bowls and garnish with **onions.**

Cooking Tip:
Try not to overcook the Brussels sprouts. They are finished cooking when they are slightly tender and have a sweet aroma, about 7-10 minutes. If using fresh, slice them in half to reduce cooking time.

Classic Italian Grilled Chicken

This simple recipe is flavored with Italian herbs and lemon juice to make a perfect compliment to any pasta dish.

Serves: 4
Approximate time: 20 minutes

Ingredients:
2 TBS olive oil
1 TBS lemon juice
1 TBS Italian seasoning *(or use recipe on pg. 90)*
2 garlic cloves, minced
salt and pepper to taste
4 (4 oz.) boneless, skinless chicken breasts, legs or thighs; or leave bone and skin in tact

Directions:
1. Combine **oil** with **lemon juice, Italian seasoning, garlic, salt** and **pepper** in a wide bowl.
2. Dip **chicken** in the oil to coat completely.
3. Spray a grill or large skillet with non-stick cooking spray and heat over medium heat.
4. Grill chicken until juices run clear, about 6 minutes per side.

Timesaving Tip:
Create enough for leftovers for a salad or top with marinara sauce (pg. 92) and serve with pasta for dinner.

Caribbean Chicken

Take your taste buds to an exotic journey with this sweet and spicy recipe.

Serves: 4
Approximate Time: 30 minutes

Ingredients:
1 (6 oz.) can pineapple slices, diced with juice
1 tsp. cornstarch, dissolved in 1 tsp cold water
1 TBS mustard
½ tsp. thyme
¼ tsp. red pepper flakes
4 (4 oz. each) boneless, skinless chicken breasts, cut into strips
3 tsp. oil
½ cup green onions, diced
2 medium bananas, sliced

Directions:
1. Drain ½ cup juice from the **pineapple**, set aside remaining juice and pineapple slices.
2. Stir **juice** and **cornstarch** mixture until smooth.
3. Stir in **mustard, thyme**, and **red pepper flakes**; set aside.
4. In a large skillet, heat **oil** over medium heat and cook **chicken strips** for 3-4 minutes or until juices run clear; remove from skillet.
5. Pour the remaining **pineapple juice** in the skillet over medium heat.
6. Add **pineapple slices** and **onion**; cook for 1 minute.
7. Stir the reserved cornstarch-pineapple juice mixture to the skillet, bring to a boil, and cook until thickens, about 1 minute.
8. Add chicken and thoroughly coat with juices; cook until heated through.
9. Turn off heat; stir in **banana slices.**

Menu Tip:
Serve over a warm cup of brown rice and a large side of spinach salad topped with mandarin slices.

Grilled Chicken Pomodoro

In Italy, cooks prepare this light and simple dish using pomodoro, which means tomato.

Serves: 4
Approximate Time: 25 minutes

Ingredients:
8 oz. rice spaghetti, uncooked
3 tsp. oil, divided
1 *each* green, red, and yellow bell peppers, seeded and sliced
2 tsp. Italian seasoning *(or use recipe on pg.90)*
 crushed red pepper, to taste
½ (3 oz.), onion, chopped
2 garlic cloves, chopped
4 (4 oz.) boneless, skinless chicken breasts, cubed *(or use leftovers from pg.43)* *
1 (14.5 oz.) can tomatoes, diced

*If using cooked chicken, slice the chicken and omit step 4

Directions:
1. Cook **pasta** according to package, until al dente; drain.
2. In a bowl combine **1 tsp. oil, bell peppers, Italian seasoning,** and **red pepper flakes.**
3. Heat **1 tsp. oil** in medium skillet over medium heat; sauté **onions** and **garlic** until tender, about 6 minutes; add to the pepper mixture in bowl.
4. Add **1 tsp. of oil** to the skillet and cook **chicken** for ten minutes, turning once.
5. Add **pepper** mixture and sauté for 2 minutes.
6. Add **tomatoes** and cook until heated through, about 2 minutes.
7. Top spaghetti with chicken mixture.

Menu Tip:
Enjoy with a side of Tuscany Broccoli (pg. 25) and Mediterranean Salad (pg. 27).

Three Ingredient Fiesta Chicken

This tasty recipe can get dinner on the table with little effort and time.

Serves: 4
Approximate Time: 15 minutes

Ingredients:
1 lb. skinless chicken tenderloins
1 cup salsa *(or use recipe on pg. 93)*
2 cups leftover cooked rice

Directions:
1. Cook **chicken** over medium-high heat in a non-stick skillet, stirring frequently for about 6 minutes or until no longer pink.
2. Add **salsa** and mix well; bring to a boil then reduce heat to medium-low; cover and simmer for 10 minutes.
3. Serve over ½ cup of **rice**.

Variation Tip:
You can elaborate this recipe by adding 1 tsp. of cumin and garnish with sliced green onions. If you don't have leftover rice, serve in warmed corn tortillas.

Chinese Chicken Salad

The tangy teriyaki sauce enhances this salad entree.

Serves: 4

Approximate Time: 15 minutes

Ingredients:

8 cups mixed greens, shredded
4 cups (1 lb.) fresh snap peas
1 cup white button, crimini or shiitake mushrooms
1 cup carrots (about 2-3), shredded
1 cup red cabbage, shredded
1 cup sweet red bell pepper (1 medium), sliced
2 cups cooked skinless chicken breast, diced
¼ cup GF teriyaki sauce *(or use recipe on pg. 92)*

Directions:

1. Toss in a large bowl the **mixed greens, snap peas, mushrooms, carrots, cabbage**, and **bell pepper.**
2. In a separate bowl mix **chicken** with **teriyaki sauce**.
3. Portion the salad mixture in 4 large bowls, top with ½ cup of teriyaki chicken.

Menu Tip:

Serve with Fried Rice (pg. 29)

Turkey With Herb and Onion Gravy

Traditional gravy calls for butter and flour, but this version is healthier and just as tasty, especially over leftover turkey slices.

Serves: 4
Approximate Time: 15 minutes

Ingredients:
1 tsp. oil
½ cup onion (3 oz.), sliced
2 TBS rice flour
2 ¼ cup broth, chicken or vegetable, divided
1 TBS thyme
1 tsp. sage
¼ tsp. pepper
   salt to taste
1 lb. cooked turkey slices

Directions
1. Heat **oil** over medium-high heat; sauté **onions** until tender, about 2 minutes,. Be careful not to brown, set aside.
2. Combine the **rice flour** in a small bowl with 1/4 cup **broth**; stir until smooth, adding additional broth if need; set aside.
3. In a saucepan, boil 2 cups of **chicken broth** over medium-low heat; reduce heat and slowly add the **rice flour mixture** into the pot, stirring constantly.
4. As gravy gently bubbles, season with **thyme, sage, pepper,** and **salt**, stirring for 2 - 3 minutes to prevent gravy from lumping.
5. Add cooked **onions** and cook until desired thickness, add more flour if needed to thicken or more broth to thin.
6. Pour generously over heated turkey slices.

Variation Tip:
You can omit the onion, if preferred, to make basic gravy.

California Turkey Wrap

The avocado and bacon add personality to a typical turkey wrap.

Serves: 4 (1 wrap each)
Approximate Time: 10 minutes

Ingredients:
¼ cup guacamole *(or use recipe on pg. 93)*
4 corn tortillas
1 cup Red leaf lettuce
½ cup bean sprouts
8 oz. turkey slices, about 8 slices
8 slices turkey bacon, cooked
1 small tomato, sliced

Directions:
1. Spread about 2 TBS of **guacamole** on each **tortilla.**
2. Place in the center of each tortilla: ¼ cup of **spinach**, 1/8 cup of **sprouts**, 2 oz. **turkey**, 2 **bacon** slices, 2 **tomatoes** and roll up the tortilla.

Cooking Tip:
A ripened avocado should yield to gentle pressure. Don't refrigerate an unripe avocado. Instead, to ripen place in a plastic bag with a banana and seal tightly. Let it sit at room temperature.

Teriyaki Bowl

Enjoy this simple and quick entrée spiked with sweet and tangy teriyaki sauce.

Serves: 4

Approximate Time: 15 minutes

Ingredients:

2 TBS oil, divided
3 garlic cloves, finely chopped
1 lb. chicken, sliced
4 cups fresh or frozen broccoli florets
2 cups white button, crimini or shiitake mushrooms
2 ½ cups carrots, peeled, sliced quarter-sized
¾ cup chicken broth
¼ cup GF teriyaki sauce *(or use recipe on pg. 92)*
1 cup brown rice, cooked

Directions:

1. Heat **1 TBS** of **oil** in skillet over medium heat; sauté the **garlic** for 30 seconds.
2. Add **chicken** and brown until juices run clear, about 4 minutes per side.
3. Set chicken aside and add the remaining **oil** to skillet and increase heat to high.
4. Stir-fry **vegetables** in **broth**, about 2 minutes.
5. Slowly add the **teriyaki sauce**, pouring on the side of the pan; stir-fry an additional 2 minutes.
6. Add chicken and cook for 2 to 3 minutes.
7. Serve over ½ cup cooked **rice**.

Variation Tip:

You can substitute beef, pork, or tofu for the chicken and you can use any selection of vegetables you want.

Enchiladas with Homemade Sauce

Short on time? You can substitute the homemade sauce with prepared sauce and save 10 minutes!

Serves: 4 (2 enchiladas each)
Approximate Time: 30 minutes

Ingredients:
2 TBS oil
¼ cup onion, finely chopped
1 garlic clove, crushed
1 (8 oz.) can tomato sauce
¼ cup water
2 tsp. ground cumin
½ tsp. oregano
1 tsp. cayenne red pepper
½ tsp. *each* salt and pepper
1 TBS cornstarch dissolved in 1TBS cold water
8 corn tortillas
2 cups cooked shredded chicken, pork, or beef
1 ¼ cups soy shredded cheese

Directions:
1. Preheat oven to 375 degrees F. and spray a baking dish with non-stick spray.
2. To make the sauce, heat **oil** in a saucepan over medium heat.
3. Add **onion** and **garlic;** sauté until tender, about 3 minutes.
4. Add **tomato sauce**, **water, cumin, oregano, cayenne pepper**, **salt** and **pepper**; stir to mix.
5. Stir **cornstarch** into cold water until smooth before adding to the sauce.
6. Bring the sauce to a boil, stirring constantly, then reduce heat to low and simmer for 15 minutes.
7. Stuff **corn tortillas** with ¼ cup of **chicken**, a spoonful of **enchilada sauce** and 2 TBS of **cheese**.
8. Roll up the tortilla and place seam down in the baking dish; repeat until all tortillas are stuffed.
9. Pour remaining sauce over the tortillas and sprinkle with remaining **cheese**.
10. Cover with foil and bake for 15 minutes or until heated through.

Variation Tip:
You can add chopped green onions at the last five minutes of baking.

Spicy Soft Tacos

A flavorful dinner that you can eat with your hands!

Serves: 4
Approximate Time: 15 minutes

Ingredients:
1/3 cup tomato, diced
1 TBS lime juice
3 tsp. chili seasoning *(or use recipe on pg. 89)*
2 cups cooked chicken, beef, or turkey, shredded
3 cups lettuce, thinly sliced
¼ cup red onion, finely chopped
8 corn tortillas, warmed *(see tip below)*

Directions:
1. Thoroughly mix in **tomatoes, lime juice**, and **seasoning** until heated through in a large non-stick skillet over medium heat.
2. Add cooked **meat.**
3. Warm **corn tortillas**.
4. Divide **lettuce, onion**, and **chicken** in each tortilla; fold over and serve with guacamole (pg. 93) or salsa (pg. 93), if desired.

Tip:
Warm tortillas (Ovens may vary. Adjust cooking times until tortillas are warm and flexible.)

Microwave: Stack between paper towels and microwave on High 10 to 15 seconds.

Oven: Preheat oven to 375 degrees F. and wrap each tortilla in foil and cook for 10 minutes or until warm and flexible.

Skillet: Place individual tortillas in a dry skillet over medium heat until warm and flexible.

Sloppy José

The is a Mexican version of the classic Sloppy Joe recipe. Add hot pepper sauce for even more kick.

Serves: 4
Approximate Time: 30 minutes

Ingredients:
1 lb. ground turkey, beef, or pork
¼ cup chopped onion (*about 1 small*)
¼ cup diced green pepper, (*about 1 small*)
¼ cup sliced celery (*about 1 stalk*)
¾ cup ketchup
1 tsp. brown mustard
1 tsp. Worcestershire sauce
¼ tsp. paprika
¼ tsp. garlic powder
   salt and pepper to taste
8 slices Gluten Free bread

Directions:
1. Over medium heat, brown **meat** in large skillet with **onions, bell pepper**, and **celery**, for about 5 minutes, or until onion is tender.
2. Add **ketchup, mustard,** and **Worcestershire sauce, paprika**, and **garlic**; mix well.
3. Reduce heat and simmer for 20 minutes; season with **salt** and **pepper.**
4. Serve between two slices of gluten free **bread** or inside a large lettuce leaf; garnish with fresh parsley leaves.

Menu Tip:
Serve these with Stove Top Rosemary Potatoes on page 24.

Savory Meatballs

This recipe is perfect for those who suffer from multiple food allergies. Although it omits breadcrumbs, eggs, and cheese, the dynamic flavor of dried herbs and seasonings makes these meatballs delicious!

Serves: 4 (6 meatballs, ¼ cup sauce)
Approximate Time: 25 minutes

Ingredients
1 lb. ground turkey or lean beef
1 tsp. dried onion flakes
1 tsp. garlic powder
1 tsp. basil
1 tsp. oregano
1 tsp. parsley
1 tsp. salt
1 TBS GF Worcestershire sauce
1 TBS oil
1 cup marinara sauce *(or use recipe on pg. 92.)*

Directions:
1. Combine **turkey** with **onion, garlic, basil, oregano, parsley, salt,** and **Worcestershire Sauce** in a medium bowl.
2. Form 24 meatballs.
3. Heat **oil** in a skillet over medium heat; add meatballs, turning to coat in oil.
4. Move the pan around for about 5 minutes to brown all sides until no longer pink inside. Check to see if it is done, by cutting one open.
5. Carefully pour **marinara sauce** over the meatballs and simmer on medium-low for 15 minutes.

Menu Tip:
Serve this over warm rice pasta with a side salad of fresh mixed greens drizzled with Italian dressing or use recipe on page 91.

Chili with Beans

Warm up with a big bowl of spicy and hearty chili on a cold, wintry night.

Serves: 4 (1 cup)
Approximate Time: 30 minutes

Ingredients:
½ lb. ground turkey or beef
1 cup onion (1 large), chopped
2 garlic cloves, minced
½ cup green pepper (1 medium), chopped
1 (15 oz.) can tomato sauce
1 (15 oz.) can of diced tomatoes, with juice
1 (10 oz) can kidney beans, rinsed and drained
1/8 tsp. cumin
½ tsp. chili powder
½ tsp. oregano
dash of red pepper flakes

Directions:
1. In a large saucepan, brown the **meat, onion, garlic,** and **pepper** over low heat; drain the fat.
2. Add the remaining ingredients; stir to combine.
3. Bring to a boil, reduce heat, and simmer uncovered for 15-20 minutes.

Variation Tip:
This can also be a vegetarian meal by replacing the meat with an additional 2 cups of beans.

Ratatouille

This authentic French cuisine can dress up any type of meat.

Serves: 4
Approximate Time: 5 minutes

Ingredients:
1 TBS oil
4 cups eggplant, (about 1 medium)
1/2 cup onion (about 1 medium), thinly sliced
1/2 cup green pepper (about 1 medium), thinly sliced
1 (4 oz.) can mushrooms, drained
3 garlic cloves, minced
1 (15.5 oz.) can tomatoes, diced
¼ cup water
1 tsp. basil
½ tsp. oregano
¼ tsp. thyme
   salt and pepper to taste

Directions:
1. Heat **oil** over medium-high heat in a nonstick skillet.
2. Add **eggplant,** stirring occasionally about 3 minutes or until golden at edges and begins to soften in the middle.
3. Add **onion, bell pepper, mushrooms,** and **garlic,** stirring for 5 minutes or until slightly tender.
4. Stir in **tomatoes**, **water**; **basil, oregano** and **thyme,** cover and simmer for 10 minutes or until vegetables are tender. Add more water if needed.

Variation Tip:
Enjoy this over grilled chicken or fish.

Mushroom-Onion Burgers on Leaf Wraps

This breadless burger is so tasty with the sweet onion topping, you wont miss the bun

Serves: 5
Approximate Time: 20 minutes

Ingredients:
1 lb. ground turkey, chicken, pork, or lean beef
3 tsp. Worcestershire sauce, divided
¼ tsp. garlic powder
¼ tsp. pepper
¼ tsp. paprika
1 (4 oz.) can mushrooms, drained
½ cup onion thinly sliced
4 large romaine leaves

Directions:
1. Mix **ground meat** with **1 tsp. Worcestershire sauce, garlic powder, pepper,** and **paprika**; roll into 4 equal rounds.
2. Heat a grill or a skillet over medium heat and cook meat patties until cooked through, browning on both sides, about 5 minutes per side; remove from skillet.
3. With meat juices, add remaining **Worcestershire sauce, mushrooms,** and **onions**; sauté for 5 minutes or until onions are very soft.
4. Place a burger on each
5. Pour onion mixture on top.

Menu Tip:
Serve this with Roasted Asparagus on page 21 and a tall glass of chilled Apple Pie Cider on page 86.

Beef and Herb Potato Skillet

This hearty dinner is a healthier variation of store-bought frozen entrees.

Serves: 4
Approximate Time: 30 minutes

Ingredients:
1 cup beef broth
2 TBS barbecue sauce or ketchup
1 TBS Dijon mustard
1 TBS cornstarch
1 lb. potatoes (cut into wedges)
½ tsp. garlic salt
1 TBS Italian seasoning *(or use recipe on pg. 92)*
1 1/2 cups green beans, fresh or frozen *(see tip below)*
1 cup sliced carrots, (about 3) fresh or frozen
1 cup celery, (about 2 stalks)
1/4 cup water
1 TBS oil
1/4 tsp. *each* salt and pepper
1 lb. sirloin tip (about 1" thick) sliced into 2-inch pieces

Directions:
1. Preheat oven to 400 degrees F.
2. Coat a large baking sheet with nonstick cooking spray.
3. Whisk **broth, sauce, mustard**, and **cornstarch**; set aside.
4. Place **potatoes** on baking sheet and sprinkle with **garlic salt** and **seasoning**; bake for 20 minutes or until tender.
5. Meanwhile, in a large skillet over medium high combine **green beans**, **carrots**, **celery** and **water**; cover and cook for 5 minutes.
6. Remove lid and cook until water evaporates; remove vegetables from pan and set aside.
7. Heat **oil** in skillet over medium-high heat.
8. Sprinkle **salt** and **pepper** on **sirloin** and add to skillet; cook for 3 to 4 minutes.
9. Pour broth mixture into skillet; boil for 1 minute or until thickened.
10. Add vegetables and potatoes; mix well in broth.

Timesaving Tip:
Use frozen veggies to save preparation time, but if using fresh green beans, trim the ends off first.

Tri-Pepper Beef Fajitas

You can bring home the southwestern flavor with this sizzling dish.

Serves: 4 (8 fajitas)
Approximate Time: 25 minutes

Ingredients:
1 lb. flank steak
3 tsp. fajita seasoning *(or use recipe on pg. 90)*
1 TBS oil
1 of *each* medium red, green, and yellow bell pepper, seeded and thinly sliced
1 large onion, thinly sliced
1 large tomato, sliced into wedges.
1 TBS lemon juice
8 corn tortillas

Directions:
1. Cut **steak** into ¼ inch strips: mix with **seasoning**; set aside.
2. Heat **oil** in a large skillet over medium-high heat; sauté **peppers**, **onion**, and **tomatoes**, stirring constantly for about 4 minutes.
3. Add **lemon juice** mix well.
4. Add steak and cook until heated through, about 4 minutes.
5. Serve in warmed **tortillas.**

Menu Tips:
Top with guacamole *(pg. 93)* and salsa *(pg. 93)* with a spinach salad mixed with grilled corn kernels and sun-dried tomatoes.

Roast Beef Wrapped Asparagus

This can be served as a cold appetizer or double the recipe to serve as a warm main dish with a side of rice and steamed vegetables.

Serves 4 (2 slices each)
Approximate Time: 15 minutes

Ingredients:
24 asparagus spears, woody ends trimmed
1 tsp. oil
¼ tsp. garlic powder
¼ tsp. chives
¾ lb deli roast beef, or 8 slices
4 TBS lemon mustard dressing *(or use recipe on pg. 91)*

Directions:
1. Preheat oven to 450 degrees F, spray non-stick cooking spray in a baking dish.
2. Boil the **asparagus** for 2-3 minutes or until softened. (*See tip below*)
3. Mix **oil** with **garlic** and **chives**; set aside.
4. Wrap **roast beef slices** around 3 spears.
5. Arrange in baking dish, seam side down.
6. Pour oil mixture on top.
7. Bake for 10-12 minutes or until asparagus is tender.
8. Serve with lemon mustard dressing drizzled on top, if desired.

Cooking Tip:
To keep the asparagus bright green, boil less then 3 minutes, then immediately immerse in ice cold water. Drain and blot dry.

Broccoli and Sausage Pasta

Enjoy this heart friendly meal by switching turkey sausage for pork.

Serves: 4
Total time: 30 minutes

Ingredients:
12 oz. spaghetti pasta, or any gluten-free pasta of choice
4 cups broccoli florets, fresh or frozen
4 (3 oz.) Italian turkey sausages, thinly sliced
1 pt. grape tomatoes, cut in half
2 tsp. basil
   salt and pepper to taste

Directions:
1. Cook **pasta** according to package.
2. Add **broccoli** when 3 minutes of cooking time remain.
3. Drain, reserving ½ cup of cooking water
4. Meanwhile, over medium heat cook **sausage** slices in a large nonstick skillet for 7-8 minutes or until golden brown.
5. Add **tomatoes, basil, salt** and **pepper**; cook 5 minutes, frequently stirring.
6. Add ¼ cup pasta water, broccoli, and pasta to sausage in skillet; heat through adding additional water if needed.
7. Remove from heat; serve immediately.

Time Saving Tip:
Double the recipe to make leftovers for next day lunch.

Pepper-Jack Polenta Pizza

You don't have to give up pizza with this delicious gluten and dairy-free recipe.

Serves: 6 (1 slice each)

Approximate Time: 20 minutes

Ingredients:

2 ¼ cups water
½ **cup** of instant polenta
½ **tsp.** salt
2 **tsp.** olive oil
1 garlic clove, minced
½ **cup** sliced onion
½ **cup** mushrooms
¼ **cup** diced green bell pepper
½ **cup** prepared marinara sauce *(or use recipe on pg. 92)*
12 slices turkey pepperoni
1 medium tomato, thinly sliced
½ **cup** shredded soy pepper jack cheese

Directions:

1. Preheat oven to 450 degrees F.
2. To make the curst, boil the **water**. Add the **polenta** and **salt** and whisk until fully mixed; reduce heat and continue stirring for 3 to 5 minutes until the batter thickens.
3. Pour into a 9" prepared pie pan, cover with plastic wrap, and chill in the fridge until room temperature.
4. As the crust chills, heat the **oil** in a skillet over medium-high heat and sauté the **garlic** for 30 seconds, then add the **onion, mushrooms,** and **green pepper** until the onion is tender, about 2 minutes.
5. Pour the **marinara sauce** over the crust, then top with **onions, mushrooms, pepper, tomato,** and **pepperoni**; bake 8 minutes.
6. Sprinkle the **cheese** and bake until the cheese melts, about 2 minutes.
7. Cut into 6 slices.

Variation Tip:

Make this vegetarian by omitting the pepperoni and add extra cheese and veggies.

Garlicky-Lemon Salmon and Tomatoes

Want to entice your taste buds in less then twenty minutes?

Serves: 4 (1 fillet, 1/2 tomato)
Approximate Time: 15 minutes

Ingredients:
¼ **cup** water or broth
2 large tomatoes
4 (6 oz.) salmon steaks
2 TBS oil
½ **TBS** paprika
1 TBS lemon salt
   salt and pepper to taste
4 tsp. thyme
4 garlic cloves, sliced

Directions:
1. Heat broiler.
2. Pour **water** or **broth** in a roasting pan.
3. Slice **tomatoes** in half; place cut-side up in a roasting pan.
4. Add **salmon.**
5. Drizzle **oil** over salmon and tomatoes; season with **paprika, lemon salt, salt**, **pepper**, **thyme** and **garlic**.
6. Broil until salmon is opaque and tomatoes are tender, about 8 to 10 minutes.

Menu Tip:
Serve this with Cranberry-Walnut Wild Rice on page 28.

Fast Mediterranean Fish Stew

This seafood dish is so fast to prepare, but the taste will linger.

Serves: 4
Approximate Time: 20 minutes

Ingredients:
1 TBS oil
½ cup onion (about 1 small) cut into wedges
1 garlic clove finely minced
1 (14.5 oz) can stewed tomatoes
½ cup water
1 medium bell pepper, cut lengthwise
1 cup sliced button mushrooms
½ tsp. oregano
¼ tsp. salt
 black pepper to taste
4 (6 oz.) skinless tilapia fillets, cubed

Directions:
1. Heat **oil** in a large skillet over medium heat; add **onion** and **garlic** and stir for 2 to 3 minutes, or until the onion is tender.
2. Add undrained **tomatoes, water, bell pepper, mushrooms, oregano, salt** and **pepper;** bring to a boil, then reduce heat and simmer for 5 minutes, or until the bell peppers are tender.
3. Gently add the **fish** cubes on top; cover and simmer for 5 to 6 minutes, or until the fish flakes easily.
4. With a wide spoon, fill 4 large bowls with equal amount of stew.

Variation Tip:
You can substitute this recipe with any variety of white fish, such as flounder, halibut, cod, or sole.

Paprika Fish

You can use this spicy rub on any type of white fish.

Serves: 4
Approximate Time: 20 minutes

Ingredients:
1 TBS oil, divided
4 (4-6 oz. each) white fish fillets, fresh or frozen *(see tip below)*
2 TBS paprika rub *(or use recipe on pg. 90)*

Directions:
1. Heat 1/2 TBS **oil** in skillet over medium-high heat; place fillets and cook for 4 minutes.
2. Brush remaining **oil** on top and sprinkle **paprika** mixture on each **fish**.
3. Cook for 10-13 minutes for frozen or 6-8 minutes for fresh, or until fish is opaque throughout.

Cooking Tip:
Rinse ice glaze from frozen fish under cold water and pat dry with a towel before adding to the skillet.

Roasted Zucchini and Fish

You can roast with any white-fleshed fish to make this flavorful dish.

Serves: 4
Approximate time: 25 minutes

Ingredients:
¼ **cup** water
2 TBS lemon juice
1 TBS oil
1 ½ tsp. oregano
½ tsp lemon pepper seasoning
¼ **tsp** salt
¼ **tsp** pepper
1 lemon, peeled and thinly sliced
4 (4 oz.) tilapia fillets
1 lb. zucchini (about 3 medium), sliced
3 garlic cloves, sliced

Directions:
1. Preheat oven to 375 degrees F.
2. Mix **water, lemon juice, oil, oregano, lemon pepper seasoning, salt,** and **pepper** in a 13"x 9" baking dish; place the **lemon slices** in the pan.
3. Add the **tilapia** and flip twice to coat well with mix, then place on top of the lemon slices.
4. Slice the **zucchini** and stir in the mixture; sprinkle **garlic.**
5. Roast, stirring the zucchini up to two times for 15 to 20 minutes or until the fish flakes easily.
6. Serve with lemon slices and drizzle with remaining pan juices.

Cooking Tips:
Lemon slices keep the white fish from sticking to the pan.

Quinoa Shrimp Salad

This salad can be assembled in ten minutes with leftover quinoa or thirty minutes if you have to cook the quinoa. Either way, you will have a satisfying dinner in no time!

Serves: 4
Approximate Time: 10- 30 minutes

Ingredients:
24 oz. shrimp, precooked and thawed
3 tsp. oil
3 tsp. Italian seasoning *(or use recipe on pg. 90)*
½ tsp. garlic powder
2 cups water, if using dry quinoa or **1/2 cup** for cooked
1 cup dry quinoa, or 3 ¾ cooked *(if using cooked, see step 2)*
8 cups spinach

Directions:
1. Mix **shrimp** with **oil, Italian seasoning,** and **garlic**; set aside.
2. Meanwhile, bring **water** and **quinoa** to a boil, then reduce to low, cover and simmer, stirring occasionally until water is absorbed, about 10 minutes. If using cooked quinoa, add 1/2 cup of water and reheat in a saucepan and continue with the following steps.
3. Remove from heat and allow it to sit for 5 minutes with the cover on.
4. Arrange spinach on 4 plates, and evenly top each plate with quinoa and shrimp.

Variation Tip:
If you like more dressing, sprinkle about 1 TBS of red wine vinegar on each serving after arranging plates.

Mediterranean Tuna Wrap

Enjoy this bread-free, guilt-free wrap with a Mediterranean Salad on page 27.

Serves: 4
Total Time: 12 minutes

Ingredients:
2 (6 oz.) can chunk light tuna, drained
¼ cup red onion (1/2 small), finely diced
3 TBS parsley
¼ cup chopped Kalamata olives
2 TBS oil
1 TBS freshly squeeze juice
salt and pepper to taste
4 lettuce leaves, large
1 medium tomato, sliced

Directions:
1. In a large bowl, combine **tuna**, **onion**, **parsley**, and **olives**.
2. In a small bowl, stir **oil, lemon juice, salt and pepper**.
3. Pour the dressing over the tuna mixture and toss to combine.
4. Scoop the tuna mixture on the **leaves**; top with **tomato** slices.

Nutritional Tip:
The Mediterranean diet is heart healthy with the abundant use of olive oil and the omega-3 from the fish.

Quinoa Stuffed Peppers

This dish can be served as a side dish or enjoyed as a vegetarian main dish with a side salad.

Serves: 4

Approximate Time: 30 minutes

Ingredients:
- 2 **TBS** oil
- 1 **cup** onion, finely chopped
- 3 garlic cloves, minced
- 1 (**4 oz**.) **can** sliced mushrooms
- 1 **TBS** chile powder
- 1 **tsp**. salt
- 1 (**14.5 oz**) **can** crushed tomatoes with juice
- ¾ **cup** water
- ½ **cup** dry quinoa
- 4 **large** green peppers, tops and seeds removed
- 1 (**15 oz**.) **can** black beans, drained and rinsed

Directions:
1. Preheat oven to 350 degrees F.
2. Heat **oil** over medium heat and sauté **onions** for 3-5 minutes or until translucent.
3. Add **garlic** and drained **mushrooms** and sauté about 5 minutes.
4. Stir in **chili powder, salt**, **tomatoes,** and **wate**r, and **quinoa.**
5. Reduce heat, cover and simmer for 20 minutes, stirring occasionally.
6. Meanwhile, boil a large pot of water; add bell peppers and boil for five minutes; drain.
7. Combine **beans** with prepared **quinoa**; stuff in peppers and stand upright in baking dish; cover and bake for 15 minutes or until green peppers are tender.

Timesaving Tip:
You can reduce the preparation time by using leftover cooked quinoa or any other rice. Just add the rice with the tomatoes after step 4 and simmer for 5 minutes.

Southwestern Bean Burritos

Growing up in the southwest, this burrito was my favorite.

Serves: 4
Approximate Time: 10 minutes

Instruction:
1 tsp. oil
2 garlic cloves, minced
1 cup zucchini, diced
1 (14. 5 oz.) can tomatoes, diced
1 (14.5 oz.) can black or pinto beans, rinsed
1/8 tsp. cayenne pepper
1/2 tsp. cumin
2 TBS cilantro
8 corn tortillas
1/2 cup shredded lettuce
3 green onion, chopped
1/2 avocado, thinly sliced
1/2 cup salsa
*(or use recipe on page 94)

Directions:
1. Heat **oil** in a large skillet over medium heat and sauté **garlic** until tender.
2. Add **zucchini** and stir for 5 minutes.
3. Add **tomatoes** and **beans**; reduce heat and cook until heated through, about 1 minute.
4. Add **cayenne, cumin,** and **cilantro**; mix well.
5. Serve in warm **corn** tortillas, topped with shredded **lettuce, green onion**, **avocado** and garnish with **salsa**.

Time Saving Tip:
If you are short on time, omit the zucchini and add 1 cup of frozen corn.

Moroccan Chickpea Stew

This simplified, flavorful stew uses a variety of spices to create an exotic aromatic blend.

Serving: 4
Total Time: 30 minutes

Ingredients:

1 TBS olive oil
2 cups chopped red, yellow, or green bell peppers
2 cups zucchini, cut into 2-inch cubes
1 ½ cups chopped onion
2 tsp. ground cinnamon
½ tsp. cumin
½ tsp. ginger
1 tsp. pepper
¼ tsp. of salt
1 (15.5 oz.) can chickpeas (garbanzo bean) drained and rinsed
1 (14.5 oz.) can diced tomatoes, with juice
1 cup water

Directions:

1. Heat **oil** in a 3 quart saucepan on medium-high heat. sauté the **bell peppers, zucchini,** and **onions** until the vegetables are soft, about 5 minutes.
2. Add the **cinnamon, cumin, ginger, pepper**, and **salt,** stirring for one minute.
3. Stir in the **beans, tomatoes,** and **water** and bring to a boil; reduce heat to medium-low, cover and simmer for 20 minutes until zucchini is tender.

Menu Tip:

End you meal with a fresh cup of Moroccan Mint Tea. Pour hot water in a tea pot; combine 4 green tea bags, 5 sprigs of mint, and 2 TBS of sugar and allot to brew for 3 minutes. Stir the sugar before pouring into 4 mugs.

Quickest Beans and Rice Meal

When you are hungry and you have only 5 minutes to spare, enjoy this Tex-Mex dish in one step!

Serves: 4 (1 cup each)
Approximate Time: 5 minutes

Ingredients:

3 cups leftover rice

1 (15. 5 oz) can black beans, rinsed and drained

1 cup salsa *(or use recipe on pg. 93)*

Directions:
1. Combine **rice, beans,** and **salsa** in a saucepan over medium heat; cover and cook for 5 minutes or until heated through; add water if it is too dry.
2. Enjoy! I just had to add another step!

Variation Tip:

When you have a little more time, sauté minced garlic with ½ bell pepper and ½ onion until tender, then add the beans, rice, and salsa.

Mini Spinach-Mushroom Quesadilla

These bite-sized quesadillas can be served as an appetizer or double the serving for a light lunch with a salad or tomato soup.

Serves: 4 (2 mini quesadillas each)
Approximate Time: 10 minutes

Ingredients:
1 tsp. oil
1 garlic glove, minced
4 cups (1 lb.) spinach, fresh or frozen *(see tip below)*
1 (**4 oz.**) **can** of mushrooms, rinsed
4 tsp. fajita seasoning *(or use recipe on pg. 90)*
1/8 tsp. black pepper
8 corn tortillas
1 cup shredded soy cheese
    salsa *(or use recipe on pg. 93)*

Directions:
1. Heat **oil** over medium heat; sauté **garlic.**
2. Add **spinach** and **mushrooms**, stirring until wilted, about 2 minutes.
3. Add **seasoning** and **pepper** and mix well
4. Scoop about ½ cup of spinach mixture in each **tortilla**.
5. Sprinkle 2 TBS **cheese** in top; fold over.
6. Place into skillet and place a plate on top to hold the quesadilla in place; flip over after 1 minute and cook the other side until crispy and cheese melts.
7. Serve with **salsa** on top.

Cooking Tip:
Thaw frozen spinach overnight in the refrigerator or defrost in the microwave. Squeeze excess water before adding.

Portobello Chili-Melt

This meaty mushroom can be eaten between two bread slices for an authentic burger-effect or served breadless with the following recipe.

Serves: 4
Approximate Time: 15 minutes

Ingredients
2 tsp. Worcestershire sauce
1 TBS extra-virgin olive oil
3 tsp. chili seasoning *(or use recipe on pg. 90)*
4 large Portobello Mushroom
salt and pepper to taste
4 slices of soy cheese
8 large lettuce leaves
1 small tomato, sliced

Directions:
1. Mix **Worcestershire sauce, oil**, and **chili seasoning** in a small bowl; drizzle on both sides of **mushrooms**.
2. Season with **salt and pepper.**
3. Warm grill or skillet to medium; place Portobello and grill for 6 to 8 minutes turning over once midway.
4. Place a slice of **cheese** on smooth side of each mushroom; allow to melt.
5. Serve on top of **lettuce leaves;** garnish with **tomato slices.**

Menu Tip:
Serve this with Onion-Pepper Sauté on page 20.

Desserts, Snacks, and Beverages

Chilled Chocolate Pudding 76
Flourless Peanut Butter Cookies 77
Grilled Pineapple with Walnut Yogurt 78
Baked Apples 79
Honey-Spiced Applesauce 80
Melon Breeze Salad 81
Nut Butter and Apple Soft Tacos 82
Tortilla Baked Chips 83
Tropical Trail Mix 84
Pizza Rice Cakes 85
Hot Apple Pie Cider 86
Masala Chai Tea Latte 87

Chilled Chocolate Pudding

This smooth, dairy-free pudding requires a lot of stirring, but it is well worth every effort.

Serves: 4 (1 cup each)
Approximate Time: 15 minutes*
*not including refrigeration time

Ingredients:
2 TBS cornstarch
2 cups vanilla flavored milk alternative, divided
3 oz. dark chocolate, broken into small pieces
2 TBS sugar or substitute

Directions:
1. Stir **cornstarch** with ½ **cup milk** in a bowl until smooth.
2. Heat remaining **milk, chocolate,** and **sugar** over medium-low heat; whisk occasionally until chocolate completely melts.
3. Increase heat to medium until mixture boils; constantly stir.
4. Stir again the cornstarch mixture until smooth before slowly adding it to the saucepan, while constantly stirring.
5. Simmer and continue to stir for 2 minutes.
6. Pour into 4 cups, cover and refrigerate for 2 hours.

Nutrition Tip:
Use organic 75% cocoa chocolate bars to take advantage of the antioxidants and soy milk for the protein and calcium.

Flourless Peanut Butter Cookies

This recipe is simple enough for the kids to bake!

Yields: 24
Approximate Time: 25 minutes

Ingredients:
1 cup peanut butter
1 ¼ cups sugar, divided
1 egg
1 tsp. baking soda
1 tsp. vanilla extract

Directions:
1. Preheat oven to 350 degrees F; line a large baking sheet with parchment paper.
2. Combine **peanut butter, 1 cup of sugar, egg, baking soda,** and **vanilla extract;** mix until smooth.
3. Drop spoonfuls of batter on baking sheet about quarter-sized, 2 inches apart.
4. Dip fork in remaining **sugar** and press crisscross designs on cookies with the back of the fork.
5. Bake 8-10 minutes or until slightly golden on top and soft in the center.
6. Allow cooling for 5 minutes before transferring to cool completely.

Menu Tip:
Serve these with a cup of Masala Chai Tea Latte on page 87.

Grilled Pineapple with Walnut Yogurt

This dessert can be cooked on the grill, but if a grill is not available, you can omit the grilling process and just serve from a skillet.

Serves: 5 (2 slices per serving)
Approximate Time: 8 minutes

Ingredients:
1 **can** pineapple slices, drained reserve **1/4 cup** of juice
1 **tsp.** cinnamon
1 **tsp.** honey
2 **cups** soy yogurt, any flavor
¼ **cup** walnuts, crushed

Directions:
1. In a skillet, bring to a boil 1/4 cup of **pineapple juice, cinnamon**, and **honey.**
2. Add **pineapple slices**, stirring juices over the slice; cook until most of the liquid is absorbed, about 5 minutes.
3. Transfer to a prepared grill or skillet and grill until grill lines form or slightly brown; remove from heat.
4. Place two slices on 5 plates; scoop ½ cup of **yogurt** on top per serving; sprinkle **walnuts** on top; pour remaining juices over slices, if desired.

Variation Tip:
You can serve this with a meal by omitting the yogurt and serve on top of cooked ham slices.

Baked Apples

Nothing tastes better than warm baked apples combined with a generous scoop of ice cream. (Lactose free, of course!)

Serves: 4 (1 apple each)
Approximate Time: 30 minutes

Ingredients:
4 large apples (Rome Beauty, Golden Delicious, or Jonagold)
½ **cup** raisins
¼ **cup** walnuts, crushed
¼ **cup** brown sugar
¼ **tsp.** nutmeg
¼ **tsp.** cinnamon
¼ **cup** apple cider or juice

Directions:
1. Preheat oven to 375 degrees F.
2. Core **apples** *(see tip below)*.
3. Combine **raisins, walnuts, sugar, nutmeg** and **cinnamon**.
4. Evenly stuff the mixture in each apple.
5. Pour **apple cider** in a deep roasting pan; place stuffed apples.
6. Bake for 20 minutes or until apples are tender.
7. Serve by pouring cider from the pan over the apples.

Cooking Tip:
If you don't have an apple corer, use a pairing knife to cut out the stem area first, then deeper into the core, almost reaching the bottom. Use a spoon to dig out the seeds. Make the hole about ¾ inches wide.

Honey Spiced Applesauce

Serve warm as a side with pork chops or chicken or serve chilled for a healthy snack.

Serves; 8
Approximate Time: 10 minutes

Ingredients:
4 cups applesauce, unsweetened
1 TBS honey
½ tsp. cinnamon
½ tsp. nutmeg
½ tsp. allspice
¼ cup walnuts, chopped, if desired

Directions:
1. Heat **applesauce** in a saucepan over medium heat.
2. Add **honey**; stir completely until melted, about 2 minutes.
3. Mix in **cinnamon, nutmeg**, and **allspice**; heat until applesauce is thoroughly warm.
4. Serve ½ cup of applesauce in small bowls; garnish with **walnuts**.

Nutrition Tip:
This can be served as low sugar substitute for syrup on top of pancakes, waffles, or French Toast (page 11). Each serving of ½ cup counts as one serving of fruit!

Melon Breeze Salad

This minty, seasonal salad is refreshing on a hot summer day.

Serves: 4 (about 1 1/4 cups)
Approximate Time: 10 minutes, not including refrigeration

Ingredients:
1 cup pineapple
1 cup seedless watermelon, (about ½ lb.)
1 cup melon, (about ½ lb.)
1 cup red grapes
1 kiwi, sliced
2 TBS of lemon juice
3 mint leaves

Directions:
1. Scoop with a melon ball **cantaloupe, watermelon,** and **melon**.
2. Sprinkle **lemon juice;** gently mix.
3. Add **mint leaves** and refrigerate until chilled, about 30 minutes to an hour; discard mint leaves when ready to serve.

Variation Tip:
Mix up the fruit by substituting seedless grapes or pineapple for the melons.

Honey Spiced Applesauce

Serve warm as a side with pork chops or chicken or serve chilled for a healthy snack.

Serves; 8
Approximate Time: 10 minutes

Ingredients:
4 cups applesauce, unsweetened
1 TBS honey
½ tsp. cinnamon
½ tsp. nutmeg
½ tsp. allspice
¼ cup walnuts, chopped, if desired

Directions:
1. Heat **applesauce** in a saucepan over medium heat.
2. Add **honey**; stir completely until melted, about 2 minutes.
3. Mix in **cinnamon, nutmeg**, and **allspice**; heat until applesauce is thoroughly warm.
4. Serve ½ cup of applesauce in small bowls; garnish with **walnuts**.

Nutrition Tip:
This can be served as low sugar substitute for syrup on top of pancakes, waffles, or French Toast (page 11). Each serving of ½ cup counts as one serving of fruit!

Melon Breeze Salad

This minty, seasonal salad is refreshing on a hot summer day.

Serves: 4 (about 1 1/4 cups)
Approximate Time: 10 minutes, not including refrigeration

Ingredients:
1 **cup** pineapple
1 **cup** seedless watermelon, (about ½ lb.)
1 **cup** melon, (about ½ lb.)
1 **cup** red grapes
1 **kiwi,** sliced
2 **TBS** of lemon juice
3 mint leaves

Directions:
1. Scoop with a melon ball **cantaloupe, watermelon,** and **melon**.
2. Sprinkle **lemon juice;** gently mix.
3. Add **mint leaves** and refrigerate until chilled, about 30 minutes to an hour; discard mint leaves when ready to serve.

Variation Tip:
Mix up the fruit by substituting seedless grapes or pineapple for the melons.

Nut Butter and Apple Soft Tacos

This quick and healthy snack adds a little pizzazz to apples and peanut butter.

Serves: 4 (1 taco each)
Approximate Time: 5 minutes

Ingredients:
4 corn tortillas
½ cup nut butter, almond or peanut butter
1 apple, thinly sliced
4 tsp. honey

Directions:
1. Heat **tortillas.** *(see page 52 for tips)*
2. Spread 1 TBS **nut butter** on each tortilla.
3. Fill evenly with **apple slices**.
4. Sprinkle **cinnamon** and drizzle **1 tsp. of honey** on each serving.

Variation Tip:
You can substitute the apple for other fruits, such as pears, bananas, or strawberries.

Tortilla Baked Chips

These bite-sized snacks are so versatile. See tip below for topping options to the basic recipe.

Yields: 40 chips
Approximate Time: 20 minutes

Ingredients:
1 **TBS** oil
½ **tsp** salt
5 corn tortillas

Directions:
1. Preheat oven to 400 degrees F.
2. Pour **oil** in a bowl and sprinkle **salt**.
3. Stack the **corn tortillas** on top of each other; use a pizza cutter to slice into eighths.
4. Toss the tortilla wedges into the bowl and toss until covered with salt.
5. Spray non-stick cooking spray on a baking sheet; evenly layer the wedges on the sheet about ¼ inch apart and bake for 10-15 minutes or until chips are beginning to get crispy and brown at the edges.
6. Remove from oven and cool 5 to 10 minutes or until crispy.

Variation Tip:
Options for toppings: Paprika, chili powder, cumin, garlic powder, cayenne pepper, or try a sweet version with cinnamon and sugar.

Tropical Trail Mix

The crunchy blend of seeds, nuts, and dried fruits creates a satisfying snack for on-the-go people.

Serves: 12 (1/4 cup)
Approximate Time: 10 minutes

Ingredients:
½ **cup** macadamia cuts
½ **cup** sunflower seeds
½ **cup** dried cranberries
½ **cup** raisins
½ **cup** GF rice cereal
½ **cup** chopped coconut

Directions:
1. Mix and portion out into ¼ cup servings.
2. Store in an airtight container up to two weeks.

Cooking Tip:
You can use any variety of mixtures using equal parts of nuts and seeds, dried fruits, and GF cereal or chocolate.

Pizza Rice Cakes

A simple, crispy pizza version can be served as a snack or a light lunch with a salad.

Serves: 4
Approximate Time: 5 minutes

Ingredients:
¼ **cup** marinara sauce *(or use recipe on pg. 92)*
4 rice cakes
4 slices of soy cheese

Directions:
1. Preheat broiler.
2. Spread 2 TBS of **marinara sauce** on each **rice cakes.**
3. Place **cheese slices** on top.
4. Place under broiler and cook until cheese melts (about 3 minutes).

Variation Tip:
Go crazy with the toppings; add fresh mushrooms, spinach leaves, etc., and broil for 3 minutes or until veggies are tender, then top with cheese and broil until cheese melts.

Hot Apple Pie Cider

On a cold, crisp day, warm up with a cider that tastes like a piece of apple pie.

Serves: 6 (1 cup)
Approximate Time: 15 minutes

Ingredients:
6 cups apple cider
1 **tsp.** vanilla extract
1 **TBS** honey
1 **TBS** cinnamon
½ **tsp.** allspice
¼ **tsp.** nutmeg

Directions:
1. Combine the **cider, vanilla**, and **honey** in a pot over medium-high; stir until honey dissolves.
2. Place the **cinnamon, allspice,** and **nutmeg** in a cheesecloth; fold the corners into a bundle, then tie up with a string; place in the cider.
3. Simmer for 5 to 10 minutes or until cider is very hot but not boiling.
4. Discard the bundle and pour into 6 cups; garnish with a cinnamon stick.

Variation Tip:
Use this cider as a liquid base for Baked Apples on page 79 or poached pears.

Masala Chai Tea Latte

Masala means spice and chai means tea in Hindi, which is a traditional drink of India and a soothing alternative to coffee.

Serves: 4
Approximate Time: 15 minutes

Ingredients:
4 cups fresh, filtered cool water
4 black tea bags, decaf or regular
1 tsp. cinnamon
½ tsp. ginger
¼ tsp. nutmeg
¼ tsp. cardamom
¼ tsp. black pepper
2 TBS sugar or honey, if desired
2 cups vanilla flavored milk alternative, or more for the liking

Directions:
1. In a large saucepan bring **water** just to a boil, reduce heat and add **tea bags**; simmer for 5 minutes.
2. Meanwhile combine **cinnamon, ginger, nutmeg, cardamom**, and **black pepper** in a cheese cloth, fold to bunch and tie with a string.
3. Remove tea bags.
4. Add **sugar** or **honey** to tea; mix until completely dissolved, about 1 minute.
5. Place cheesecloth spices in the pot and simmer 10 minutes.
6. Remove the bag and add the **milk alternative** and cook until the tea is hot again.
7. Remove from heat and immediately pour in 4 mugs; garnish with a cinnamon stick.

Cooking Tip:
Don't overcook the tea bags because tea leaves can taste too bitter when exposed to hot water beyond 5 minutes.

Seasonings, Sauces, and Dressings

Chili Seasoning 89
Cajun Seasoning 89
Italian Seasoning 90
Fajita Seasoning 90
Paprika seasoning 90
Lemon Mustard Dressing 91
Honey Mustard Dressing 91
Mediterranean Dressing 91
Italian Dressing 91
Marinara Sauce 92
Teriyaki Sauce 92
Guacamole 93
Salsa 93

Seasonings

Combine all ingredients and store tightly in a jar. If buying fresh herbs, the rule of thumb is 1 tablespoon of fresh per teaspoon of dried. Use ¼ teaspoon of the mixture per serving.

Chili Seasoning
Yields: ¼ cup

Ingredients:
1 TBS ground cumin
1 TBS paprika
1 tsp. dried oregano
¼ tsp. chili
¼ tsp. cinnamon

Tip:
Use for Mexican or Spanish dishes.

Cajun Seasoning
Yields ¼ cup

Ingredients:
2 tsp. white pepper
2 tsp. garlic powder
2 tsp. onion powder
2 tsp. ground red pepper
2 tsp. paprika
2 tsp. black pepper

Tip:
Use over meat, rice, and potatoes

Italian Seasoning
Yields ½ cup

Ingredients:
2 **TBS** dried basil
2 **TBS** dried marjoram
1 **TBS** garlic powder
1 **TBS** oregano
1 **TBS** thyme
1 **TBS** rosemary

Tip:
Use on any Italian dish.

Fajita Seasoning:
Yields: 1 cup

Ingredients:
2 TBS cumin
4 tsp pepper
4 tsp oregano
2 tsp garlic powder
1/3 cup chili powder
½ cup dried minced onion

Tip:
Use as a substitute for taco seasoning.

Paprika Seasoning
Yields: ¼ cup

Ingredients:
1 TBS paprika
1 ½ tsp oregano
1 tsp garlic powder
1 tsp pepper
½ tsp cayenne pepper, less for milder taste

Tip:
Use as a dry rub for poultry, beef, and fish

Dressing

Serve over warmed vegetables or a fresh salad

Each Yields: 4 servings

Lemon-Mustard Dressing

Ingredients:
2 TBS plain soy yogurt
1 TBS sweet brown mustard
1 TBS lemon juice
1 tsp. grated lemon zest

Directions:
Mix yogurt with brown mustard and lemon juice;

Honey Mustard Dressing

Ingredients:
2 1/2 TBS honey
1 1/2 TBS Dijon mustard
1 TBS rice wine vinegar

Directions:
Combine all ingredients and whisk until smooth.

Mediterranean Dressing

Ingredients:
3 TBS extra virgin olive oil
1 tsp. lemon juice
½ tsp. oregano
½ tsp. basil
2 garlic cloves, minced
  sea salt and pepper to taste

Directions:
   Mix all ingredients until fully mixed

Italian Dressing

Ingredients:
4 tsp. Italian seasoning (pg. 90)
4 TBS oil

Directions:
Mix well.

Sauces

Bake large batches to store in an airtight glass container up to 1 week in the refrigerator.

Marinara Sauce
Yields: about 3 cups

Ingredients:
1 **tsp.** oil
3 garlic cloves, minced
1 **(28 oz.) can** crushed tomatoes
3 **tsp.** basil
1 **tsp.** oregano

Directions:
1. Heat **oil** in a pan over medium high; add **garlic** and sauté for 30 seconds.
2. Add **tomatoes, basil** and **oregano** and simmer for 15 minutes.

Teriyaki Sauce
Yields: 2 cups

Ingredients:
1 1/4 **cup** water, divided
¼ **cup** GF soy sauce
3 **TBS** brown sugar
1 garlic clove, minced
1 **tsp.** ginger
2 **TBS** cornstarch

Directions:
1. Combine **1 cup water, soy sauce, brown sugar, garlic** and **ginger** in a saucepan; bring to a boil.
2. Dissolve **cornstarch** in ¼ **cup cold water**; stir until smooth.
3. Slowly add to sauce, stirring constantly until sauce thickens; add more water if too thick.

Salsa
Yield: about 3 cups

Ingredients:
1 **(28 oz.)** can diced tomatoes, with juice
3 green onions, sliced
1 lime, juice
½ **tsp.** garlic salt
1 **tsp**. salt
½ **tsp.** pepper
¼ **cup** cilantro
1 **(4 oz.)** can green chilles
¼ **tsp.** cayenne powder, optional

1. Pour **tomatoes** into a blender and puree for a few seconds.
2. Add the **onion, lime juice, garlic, salt, pepper, cilantro, green chili,** and **cayenne powder**; process blender for a few seconds for chunky salsa or longer for a smoother texture.

Guacamole
Yields: 1/2 cup

Ingredients:
1 1/2 **cups** avocado pulp (about 2)
1 **TBS** lemon juice
2 **TBS** cilantro leaves, chopped
2 ½ **tsp**. cilantro
¼ **tsp.** garlic powder
¼ **tsp.** cayenne pepper
1 **tsp.** cumin

Directions:
1. Cut **avocado** in half; remove the pit (save for later) and scoop out the flesh into a bowl; mash with a fork or potato masher until desired density.
2. Add **lemon juice, cilantro, garlic powder, cayenne pepper** and **cumin.**
3. Place the pit in the center of bowl so the guacamole won't turn brown, and cover with plastic wrap and refrigerate; remove pit when ready to serve.

INDEX

Almond, *see Milk Alternatives and Nut*
Apples
    Baked Apples **79**
    Honey-Spiced Applesauce **80**
    Hot Apple Pie Cider **86**
    Nut Butter Tacos **82**
Asian, *Chinese, Japanese*
    Asian Chicken and Brussels Sprouts **42**
    Chinese Chicken Salad **47**
    Chinese Chicken Soup **37**
    Sesame Stir-Fry Green Beans **22**
    Teriyaki Bowl **50**
    Teriyaki Sauce **92**
Asparagus
    Roast Beef Wrapped Asparagus **60**
    Roasted Asparagus **21**
Avocado
    California Turkey Wrap **49**
    Guacamole **93**
Banana
    Banana-Nut Smoothie **6**
Beans
    Creamy Lentil Soup **39**
    Creamy Pea Soup **33**
    Moroccan Chickpea Stew **71**
    Quickest Beans and Rice **72**
    Quinoa Stuffed Peppers **69**
    Southwest Bean Burrito **70**
    Spicy Soft Tacos **52**
Beef *and Pork*
    Beef and Herb Potato Skillet **58**
    Chili with Beans **55**
    Enchiladas with Homemade Sauce **51**
    Mushroom-Onion Burgers **57**
    Ratatouille **56**
    Savory Meatballs **54**
    Spicy Soft Tacos **52**
    Tri-Pepper Beef Fajitas **59**
    Turkey with Herb and Onion Gravy **48**
Bell Pepper
    Onion-Pepper Sauté **20**
    Quinoa Stuffed Peppers **69**
Beverages, *Tea, Juice*
    Hot Apple Pie Cider **86**
    Masala Chai Tea Latte **87**
    Moroccan Mint Tea **71**
Broccoli
    Broccoli and Sausage Pasta **61**
    Curried Cauliflower & Broccoli Soup **40**
    Tuscany Broccoli **25**
Brussels sprouts
    Asian Chicken and Brussels Sprouts **42**
Cauliflower
    Curried Cauliflower and Broccoli Soup
Cheese, *see Milk Alternatives*
Chicken
    Asian Chicken and Brussels Sprouts **42**
    Caribbean Chicken **44**
    Chicken Noodless Soup **38**
    Chili with Beans **55**
    Chinese Chicken Soup **37**
    Classic Italian Grilled Chicken **43**
    Enchiladas with Homemade Sauce **51**
    Ratatouille **56**
    Savory Meatballs **54**

    Spicy Soft Tacos **52**
    Three Ingredient Fiesta Chicken **46**
    Turkey With Herb and Onion Gravy **48**
Chinese, *see Asian*
Cookies
    Flourless Peanut Butter Cookies **77**
Corn, *see Tortilla*
Cranberry
    Cranberry Soup **32**
    Cranberry-Walnut Wild Rice **28**
Egg
    Egg in the Window **15**
    Fast Spanish Tortilla **13**
    Quick Breakfast Burrito **12**
    The Versatile French Toast **11**
Eggplant
    Ratatouille **56**
Fish, shell fish
    Fast Mediterranean Fish **64**
    Garlicky-Lemon Salmon & Tomatoes **63**
    Mediterranean Tuna Wrap **68**
    Paprika Fish **65**
    Quinoa Shrimp Salad **67**
    Ratatouille **56**
    Roasted Zucchini and Fish **66**
Green Beans
    Sesame Stir-Fry Green Beans **22**
Italian, *see Mediterranean*
Mediterranean
    Broccoli and Sausage Pasta **61**
    Classic Italian Grilled Chicken **43**
    Grilled Chicken Pomodora **45**
    Italian Minestrone Soup **34**
    Italian Seasoning **90**
    Italian Spaghetti Squash **23**
    Marinara Sauce **92**
    Moroccan Chickpea Stew **71**
    Moroccan Mint Tea **71**
    Mediterranean Dressing **91**
    Mediterranean Salad **27**
    Mediterranean Tuna Wrap **68**
    Oven Baked Croutons **31**
    Ratatouille **56**
    Savory Meatballs **54**
    Tuscany Broccoli **25**
Melons,*Cantaloupe, Watermelon*
    Melon Breeze Salad **81**
Mexican, *Spanish, Southwest*
    California Turkey Wrap **49**
    Chili Seasoning **89**
    Chili with Beans **55**
    Enchiladas with Homemade Sauce **51**
    Fajita Seasoning **90**
    Fast Spanish Tortilla **13**
    Guacamole **93**
    Mini Spinach-Mushroom Quesadilla **73**
    Quick Breakfast Burrito **12**
    Salsa **93**
    Simple Spanish Rice **30**
    Southwest Bean Burrito **70**
    Southwestern Tofu Scramble-Toast **14**
    Spicy Soft Tacos **52**
    Spicy Tomato Soup **36**
    Three Ingredient Fiesta Chicken **46**
    Tri-Pepper Beef Fajitas **59**

Milk Alternatives, *Cheese, Milk, Yogurt*
    Banana Nut Smoothie **6**
    Chilled Chocolate Pudding **76**
    Crunchy Fruit Parfait **8**
    Grilled Pineapple w/ Walnut Yogurt **78**
    Masala Chai Tea Latte **87**
    Mini Spinach-Mushroom Quesadilla **73**
    Pepper-Jack Polenta Pizza **62**
    Pizza Rice Cake **85**
    Portobello Chili-Melt **74**

Mushroom
    Mini Spinach-Mushroom Quesadilla **73**
    Mushroom-Onion Burgers **57**
    Portobello Chili-Melt **74**

Nuts
    Apple-Nut Taco **82**
    Banana Nut Smoothie **6**
    Crunchy Fruit Parfait **8**
    Flourless Peanut Butter Cookies **77**
    Grilled Pineapple w/ Walnut Yogurt **78**
    Tropical Trail Mix **84**

Onion
    Onion-Pepper Sauté **20**
    Turkey with Herb and Onion Gravy **48**

Orange
    Orange-Strawberry Slush **7**

Peas *see Beans*
Peanut Butter, *see Nuts*
Pear
    Honey-Walnut Poached Pears **9**

Pineapple
    Caribbean Chicken **44**

Pizza
    Pepper-Jack Polenta Pizza **62**
    Pizza Rice Cakes **85**

Polenta
    Ratatouille **56**
    Pepper-Jack Polenta Pizza **62**

Pork, *see Beef*
Potato, *White, Sweet Potato*
    Cajun Sweet Potato **18**
    Stovetop Rosemary Potatoes **24**

Pumpkin
    Pumpkin Soup **35**

Quinoa
    Quinoa Breakfast Porridge **10**
    Quinoa Shrimp Salad **67**
    Quinoa Stuffed Peppers **69**

Rice, *Brown, White, Cake*
    Cranberry-Walnut Wild Rice **28**
    Fried Rice **29**
    Pizza Rice Cakes **85**
    Quickest Beans and Rice Meal **72**
    Simple Spanish Rice **30**

Salad
    Honey-Mustard Side Salad **26**
    Mediterranean Salad **27**
    Quinoa Shrimp Salad **67**

Salmon *see Fish*
Sandwiches, *Wraps*
    California Turkey Wrap **49**

Sauce *and Dressings*
    Guacamole **93**
    Honey Mustard Dressing **91**
    Italian Dressing **91**
    Lemon Mustard Dressing **91**
    Marinara Sauce **92**
    Mediterranean Dressing **91**
    Salsa **93**
    Teriyaki Sauce **92**

Sausage
    Broccoli and Sausage Pasta **61**
    Sausage Pepper -Potato Sauté **16**

Seasoning *and Spices*
    Cajun Seasoning **89**
    Chili Seasoning **89**
    Fajita Seasoning **90**
    Italian Seasoning **90**
    Paprika Seasoning **90**

Soups *and stews*
    Chicken Noodless Soup **38**
    Chinese Chicken Soup **37**
    Creamy Lentil Soup **39**
    Creamy Pea Soup **33**
    Curried Cauliflower & Broccoli Soup **40**
    Fast Mediterranean Fish **64**
    Italian Minestrone Soup **34**
    Moroccan Chickpea Stew **71**
    Pumpkin Soup **35**
    Spicy Tomato Soup **36**

Strawberry
    Orange Strawberry Slush **7**

Soy, *see Milk Alternatives*
Spanish *see Mexican*
Spices, *see Seasonings*
Spinach
    Mini Spinach-Mushroom Quesadilla **73**

Squash, *winter, Zucchini*
    Baked Acorn Squash **19**
    Italian Spaghetti Squash **23**
    Roasted Zucchini and Fish **66**

Sweet Potatoes, *see potatoes*
Tea, *see Beverages*
Teriyaki *see Asian*
Tofu
    Southwest Tofu on Toast **14**

Tomato
    Garlicky-Lemon Salmon & Tomatoes **63**
    Grilled Chicken Pomodoro **45**
    Marinara Sauce **92**
    Ratatouille **56**
    Salsa **93**
    Sloppy Jose **53**
    Spicy Tomato Soup **36**

Tortilla, *Corn*
    Nut Butter and Apple Soft Tacos **82**
    California Turkey Wrap **49**
    Tortilla Baked Chips **83**

Turkey, *see Chicken*
Walnut, *see Nuts*
Yogurt, *see Milk Alternatives*
Zucchini, *see Squash*

Find all of our recommended books at Gluten-Free & Frugal
www.glutenfreeandfrugal.com

Recommended for you...
Add these books to your library

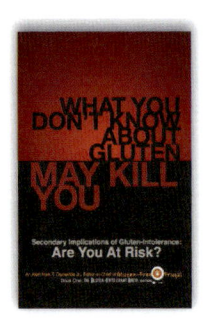

What You Don't Know About Gluten May Kill You
Secondary Implications of Gluten Intolerance
Author: T. Demeritte, Jr.
ISBN: 978-1483943817

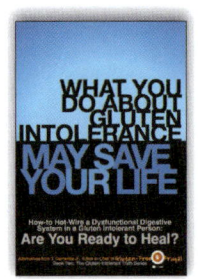

What You Do About Gluten Intolerance May Save Your Life
Book Two of the Gluten-Intolerance Truth Series
Author: T. Demeritte, Jr.
ISBN: **Coming Soon** - Register at www.glutenfreeandfrugal for release notice

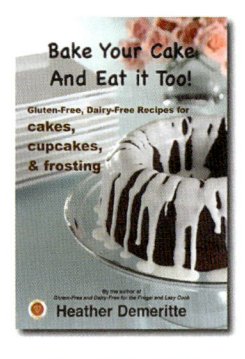

NEW COVER COMING SOON
Bake Your Gluten-Free Cake And Eat It Too!
Gluten-Free, dairy-Free Recipes for Cakes, Cupcake & Frosting
Author: Heather. Demeritte
ISBN: 9781453737541

A Gluten-Free Guide: A Letter To My Host
Help friends and family prepare safe and enjoyable meals for loved ones on a gluten free diet.
Author: Heather. Demeritte
ISBN: 9781449996642